Heirs of the Same Promise
Using Acts as a Study Guide for
Evangelizing Ethnic America

Wesley D. Balda, Editor

National Convocation on Evangelizing Ethnic America
Mission Advanced Research and Communication Center (MARC)

Acknowledgements: This book was coordinated by the
Research Task Force of Houston '85. Kn Moy and Carol Garcia
helped with building the pieces and finding contributors.
Paul Hawley proofread and Debbie Foulkes and Faith Sand
helped with editing. Monica Pyle maintained communications
between contributors and Janis Bragan Balda advised on format and
layout. Illustration by Stan Sakai, production by Suzanne Britt.

Printed in the United States of America

ISBN 0-9 1 2552-44-1   LC 84-62758

Table of Contents

Eth-nic 1. of or relating to the Gentiles or to nations not converted to Christianity. 2. having or originating from racial, linguistic and cultural ties with a specific group.

— Webster's Third New International
Dictionary, unabridged, 1971.

Preface

C. Peter Wagner *

This is a book about the *real* America.

If you speak of "Americans" to people in other lands and to significant numbers of individuals here in the U.S.A., the mental image is that of a white person of European heritage, born and brought up in a fairly comfortable home where English was always spoken, and more or less adhering to Amy Vanderbilt's standards of etiquette.

This is why it comes as a shock to many to learn that by the mid-1980s, this type of a person, known as an "Anglo," makes up only 30 percent of the American population. The other 70 percent are Asians, American Indians, Hispanics, and many others including large numbers of Europeans who feel a closer primary relationship to others of their national background than with Anglo Americans.

The real America is an increasingly complex mixture of many people groups, each with its own set of needs, each with its own cultural values, each with its own struggle for identity, and each with its own way of hearing and appropriating the gospel of Jesus Christ.

It was with this in mind that the North American Lausanne Committee proposed Houston '85, the National Convocation on Evangelizing Ethnic America. For years churches have been growing and multiplying particularly among Anglo Americans and Black Americans. But not so among most of the ethnic groups, some of which have been here for generations, such as Hispanics and Navajos and Cajun French, and some which are more recent, such as

* C. Peter Wagner
  Professor of Church Growth, Fuller Theological Seminary
  Vice-Chairman, Houston '85

1

Koreans and Iranians and Kanjobal Indians. The greatest challenge for evangelism in the U.S. today is reaching ethnics for Christ. Few American Christians realize, for example, that there are more Hispanics in te Los Angeles area alone than in seven entire Latin American nations. While the mission field is still there, it is right here on our doorstep also.

Houston '85 will deal with this issue head-on. *Heirs of the Same Promise* lays the factual and conceptual groundwork for the work of the convocation. For the first time Christian leaders from all denominations and all major ethnic groups will gather together, not to debate, but to pray and to plan. With God's help, Houston '85 will be the springboard for a harvest of souls among America's ethnic peoples even greater than many of us have dared dream for.

C. Peter Wagner

Introduction
Wesley D. Balda*

Abraham and Us

By faith Abraham, when called to go to a place he would later receive as his inheritance, obeyed and went even though he did not know where he was going. By faith he made his home in the promised land like a stranger in a foreign country; he lived in tents, as did Isaac and Jacob, who were heirs with him of the same promise. For he was looking forward to the city with foundations whose architect and builder is God. (Hebrews 11:8-10 NIV).

America abounds with ethnic diversity. Our towns and cities swell with new immigrants, and old ethnic neighborhoods maintain cultures unique to their homelands. As never before, this nation faces a rainbow of languages, colors and cultural traditions. As those who minister the gospel of Christ we are challenged and encouraged not just by the opportunity to proclaim the gospel among every people in the world, but by the undeniable fact that many of these peoples have come to live in our own neighborhoods. They are strangers in a foreign country just as Abraham was.

The scripture text is a familiar one. As readers we usually identify with Abraham. Just this time, let's pretend that we are the hosts, living in our own country. If we do this, we can see Abraham in the face of every Vietnamese refugee or undocumented Mexican laborer or Haitian sea voyager who arrives. These people are strangers in a

*Dr. Wesley D. Balda is an urban consultant with World Vision and Director of Research for the National Convocation on Evangelizing Ethnic America.

foreign country just as Abraham was. Try to imagine how Abraham felt as he journeyed through his new place.

God's word tells us that Abraham lived in tents as did Isaac and Jacob. If we've ever camped, we know that tents can be a very impermanent home. Transients live in tents, people who aren't staying in a place for very long. Tents are very vulnerable places in storms. When the weather is cold, it is harder to stay warm in a tent than it is in a house. When neighbors around a tent dweller are hostile, tents are hard to defend. Castles are much safer places for those under attack.

Or, would you like to be the only tent dweller on your block when all those who have lived in our new country a bit longer have com-

Would you like to be the only tent dweller on your block?

fortable, ranch-style homes? Even four walls and a roof, no matter how crude, are still stronger than a tent. In the cities of the Old Testament, those who lived in tents pitched them outside the city walls because there was no room inside. Those who lived in tents outside the city walls must have felt excluded and somewhat discriminated against! Many of the ethnic peoples in our country live in virtually the same way. Remember how Abraham, the tent dweller, might have felt the next time you drive through a poor barrio.

Abraham "looked forward to the city with foundations." Abraham's hope, the power of his dream, has been a stirring witness to the generations who have followed. All Americans were at one time or another strangers in a foreign country, ethnic newcomers to a land they didn't understand. Nearly every one of our ancestors came to this country with hope — because of the power of a dream. Those who are arriving in this generation or those from previous generations who maintain a unique cultural identity carry this same hope — this same powerful dream. They are Abraham to us as much as our ancestors were Abraham to those already here.

Abraham looked forward to a city with foundations. God loves the city and the city is where most of America's ethnic diversity is found. Over three quarters of *all* Americans live in urban areas and over ninety percent of ethnic America dwells in the city. Quite simply, ethnic America is urban America. We need to learn to see the city as God sees it. For Christians, this verse carries a significant teaching about the city — it is the city *with foundations.* Jesus Christ is the foundation for our lives and He can also be the foundation for our cities. We, with Abraham and with our neighbors, can look forward to cities where the foundation is Christ. Our hope and the power of our dream should be holy cities where Christ rules.

Abraham looked forward to the city with foundations *whose architect and builder is God.* We believe that God created all things and that He saw that they were good. The city was conceived in the mind of God and he created it. But like the rest of creation, it was subject to sin and death. Cities are the best opportunity God has given us for proclaiming his gospel. They are places where grace abounds, where people dwell who were created in God's image.

Abraham was "called to a place that he would later receive as an inheritance." Imagine the consternation among his hosts had they known this! And we may feel the same way, whether we have lived here for generations or have only recently arrived. Can you remember someone expressing resentment because a newcomer has developed a thriving business down the block? Are you sometimes awed by the enterprise and industry of that Southeast Asian family your church may have sponsored? What if God told you that these strangers were to receive your town as an inheritance?

There is an important lesson here for us. We do not stand alone in the light of God's favor. Other peoples will also receive the inheritance of God. We are the hosts for peoples who are heirs of the same promise that we will receive. They are brothers and sisters who will share our inheritance. How will we respond to these strangers in our country?

This book is a tool for Christians all over America. It can help you understand the changing nature of your homeland. In the end, we are all strangers in a strange land, waiting for a heavenly inheritance. Jesus has commanded us to preach the gospel to all nations. Suddenly all nations seem to be at our doorsteps!

What is this book about?

The Book of Acts is an astounding record of the church's explosion across the Roman world. The men and women of the early church ministered in cities flooded with people of different languages, cultures and religious traditions. Today, we define ethnic America as those people who see themselves as different from the dominant or media culture because of language, national origin or religious tradition. Sometimes we think no one has faced the opportunities of proclaiming the gospel to so many ethnic groups as we now view in our cities. Yet the early church did it from the first day of its existence (and did it quite well!).

This study will use Acts as a tool for looking at the challenges of evangelizing ethnic America from a biblical point of view. We have gathered articles from men and women around the nation who have much to tell us about proclaiming Christ to our neighbors. We will look at these articles through the words and actions of men and women who lived 2,000 years ago. Our goal is always to understand how we can apply what they did and learned to our own churches and neighborhoods.

Throughout this study, cross-cultural evangelism is discussed. Active, thriving ethnic churches are evangelizing others of their own ethnic group with great success around the nation. But these capable Christian leaders cannot plant churches in every neighborhood in the country. Somehow, we must all learn to understand cross-cultural America, and cross these obstacles of language, culture and religious tradition. This book is not designed just for Anglos trying to understand other cultures around them or for ethnics planting churches in their own ethnic group. It is also a call to mission for Koreans to reach Hispanics, Native Americans to reach Laotians and Filipinos to reach WASPs.

We will work through a topical study of the book of Acts. A section of readings will supplement our biblical work. The studies will explore the urban nature of ethnic America, people as whole persons, the people group idea in ethnic evangelism and ethnic ministry in our own unique situations.

How can I use this book?

This is a topical Bible study for churches, Sunday schools, missions groups and students. It can be used over several weeks during Sunday morning adult education classes, for a midweek study series or even for a special conference within a church, city or denomination.

We would especially recommend it to those planning to attend the National Convocation for Evangelizing Ethnic America in April 1985. It will prepare you for an exciting and inspiring gathering of people from around the nation at "Houston '85", as the conference is known. Acts will be the study book for this Convocation as well and this book is designed to provide a broad background for conference participants.

Write and tell us how you have used *Heirs of the Same Promise*. Our chief desire is that Christ's church would grow and that God's kingdom would be extended.

Lord, teach us to join hands and embrace all the peoples of this land with your love. Let ethnic America hear your voice!

Wesley D. Balda

Read This First

Before starting Study One, simply sit down and read through the Book of Acts. You may not have the time to do it all at once, but finish before you begin this study. Also read "The People of a New Ethnic America" by Dr. Hadaway, starting on page 41.

Then, write each of these words down on a separate 3" x 5" card and keep the terms in mind while you study:

city	town	groups
healing	Gentiles	house
synagogue	marketplace	Jews
church	priests	nation(s)
flee or fled	(city name)	temple
poor	signs & wonders	conflict

Take brief notes on each card as thoughts connected to these words spring to mind. Write the chapter and verse reference next to each note. Use more than one card per term if you need to. If a situation is related to the meaning of one of these terms, but the word itself is not used in the context, note it anyway.

Try to see the whole book as instructional for reaching people of other languages, or from other nations or religious groups for Christ. Ask yourself repeatedly, "What does this say to me right now about my neighborhood and city and what my church can do here?"

When you have read Acts and have a useful deck of note cards, sort them out on a table in front of you and begin preparing the first lesson, "STUDY ONE".

Ethnic Ministry and Cities

1

The Book of Acts is about urban evangelization of ethnic peoples and little else. The early church was urban and the network of cities throughout the Roman empire provided the vehicle for the work of Paul, Peter and other preachers and ministers of the word. Paul himself established churches in over twenty-five cities around the Mediterranean basin. When he wasn't preaching or discipling people in a city, he was traveling to the next city to start a new work there.

Some important issues reappear in urban evangelism. They are: 1) the importance of where the people are or what their context is; and, 2) the economic and racial conflict which invariably accompany the gospel message.

REFLECTION
1 — Find a concordance and count how many times the word "city", "cities" or "city's" appears in Acts. Compare this roughly to the other books of the New Testament. Any doubts left that Acts is an urban book?

2 — Read Acts 5:41-42. What two places did the apostles choose to preach?

_____   _____

Describe these particular settings as you might imagine them. Who would be there? What times of day would teaching take place? What type of dialogue might take place? What sorts of needs would the people in each setting have? Would they be Jews or Gentiles? How might the message be shaped to appeal to their needs?

_____

_____

_____

_____

_____

_____

Why do you think "house" could have a different meaning in the city? What might these houses be like?

_____

_____

_____

_____

_____

_____

3 — Now read Acts 19:8-10

The setting for preaching changed from the _____

to the _____. Why?

_____

_____

_____

What was the outcome of this change in strategy?

_____

_____

_____

Again, describe the setting using your imagination and the questions asked earlier in question 2.

_____

_____

_____

_____

4 — Now, finally, read Acts 18:6-8, 19, 26

The ministry to the Gentiles seems to be consistently placed in _____. Later, we find this to be the location for churches. If you were Paul, how would you minister in this Gentile place? What would your message be about? What needs might be found among your hearers? How could discipleship continue after you left?

_____

_____

_____

_____

_____

5 — Read Acts 13:44-45

Two key points can be found here:

1) This was mass evangelism. The whole city gathered, both Jews and others. The context was so broad that the message might have been difficult to preach. But...

2) The Jews took care of that problem! Because of their jealousy they abused Paul and Barnabas. Never the ones to be caught without a word in season, Paul and Barnabas used the situation in which they found themselves to preach. Their illustration was standing in front of them shouting rudely — what a marvelous use of drama in the church! Their sermon emphasized the conflict between the Jews and Jesus; and the Gentiles heard with joy the good news that they were included.

Find another setting from your note cards where Christians used the situation to shape the message:

_____

_____

In the setting you chose, describe why the message had more impact because of the use of the context:

_____

_____

_____

_____

6 — Read Acts 19:23-29

If you were worried that the gospel might not have economic implications in different cultures, you can now set your mind at rest. Notice in verse 27 where the priorities of Demetrius lay — first, this is going to hurt business, and then, almost as an afterthought, the goddess and the temple might be discredited. Urban ministry, because of the complexity of the structures and networks in the city, will always touch commerce and government, sometimes in painful ways.

Now, read verse 34. Not only did Paul disrupt business, but when they found out he was a Jew, an ethnic riot broke out. What is your personal assessment of Paul's response in Acts 20:1?

_____

_____

_____

_____

7 — Read Acts 16:16-24

Briefly describe the economic issue involved here:

_____

_____

_____

Again, what issue was brought up in verses 20-21?

_____

Note Paul's response in verses 39-40.

The officials asked Paul to leave the city because his presence meant economic and ethnic disruption among the Philippians. Paul stopped and enouraged the believers in Lydia's house on his way out of town. Having started a church among people of the same ethnic/cultural group he left *them* to continue the work. His departure and "passing of the mantle" effectively removed the issue of his Jewishness from the conflict. One less barrier meant that the Philippians

15

could minister among their own kind easier than Paul could. This is an example of a church started with a cross-cultural ministry, but left to grow within its own city and culture group.

APPLICATION

1 — Take the cards you have faithfully filled out and pick out verses that apply to each of the key urban issues described above. Write your interpretation of these in the spaces below next to each issue.

Gospel in Context: _____

_____

_____

_____

Economic Conflict: _____

_____

_____

_____

Ethnic/Racial Conflict: _____

_____

_____

_____

2 — There is a pattern throughout history of economic conflict leading to racial or ethnic conflict. Hitler may be an example of this. Right now there is bitter tension, and some cases of serious violence, between Vietnamese shrimp fishermen in Texas and local white fishermen. The white fishermen saw an economic issue when the Vietnamese began cutting into the profits. This led to ethnic slurs and at least one death. And this is not just an urban issue — the Texas case took place in a rural area.

Describe a similar incident you might have read about in your city's newspaper.

_____

_____

_____

_____

3 — Read the articles by Dr. Ray Bakke, page 47, and Rev. Steve Schlissel, page 89.
Have you ever thought of Jesus as one with a mixed racial heritage, as mestizo? Did you know that only 13 percent of the world is white? Write out one key idea you learned from Dr. Bakke's article that you intend to act on in the next thirty days:

_____

_____

_____

_____

Having worked through several instances of conflict between Jews and Gentiles in Acts, does Rev. Schlissel's article help you understand the contemporary scene more? Identify one Jewish acquaintance, and decide what you will do to serve that person in love during the next thirty days:

_____

_____

_____

_____

4 — Read the article "Ministering in New York City" by Bishop Golden, starting on page 113. Name each of the different settings for church planting mentioned by the author and decide why they worked:

_____

_____

_____

_____

_____

_____

_____

_____

_____

_____

_____

_____

_____

_____

_____

ACTION

1 — Set dates for completing the two actions you described in the preceding question. Be prepared to discuss your reflections on these acts after you have completed them.

_____

2 — Take the issue you described in APPLICATION question 2 and write out how you think a local church should respond to this episode:

_____

_____

_____

_____

_____

_____

Ethnic Ministry and Whole People

REFLECTION

In the Gospels, we find Jesus repeatedly disclosing himself to others through his acts. Often his credibility is established when he heals or reconciles or confronts — his words take power through his actions.

In Acts, the apostles of Jesus and their friends continue to use this same style of ministering to whole persons.

1 — Read Acts 8:5-8

"Philip went down to a city" — Philip was an urban evangelist preaching in an ethnic city. We're probably all aware that the Samaritans were an ethnic group for whom the Jews had little regard. Yet we have Philip, just one step ahead of the law (Saul the Christian-hater, in this case), preaching wherever he traveled. Philip clearly was under the impression that the gospel was also meant for other ethnic groups than his own.

The important issue here is *how* Philip proclaimed Christ. The crowds both _____ and _____ (verse 6a). We can deduce that Philip both spoke and did things. The crowd "paid close attention" because Philip's message was in deed as well as in word. Philip addressed physical infirmity and disability as well as spiritual oppression.

Think of a Christian you know who is committed to meeting the needs of the whole person. Describe a ministry encounter you're aware of involving this person's ministry:

_____

_____

_____

_____

2 — Now read Acts 9:36-43

What was Tabitha (Dorcas) known for?

_____

_____

_____

What was the consequence of Peter's ministry of healing? (verse 42)

_____

_____

_____

Read Acts 9:32-35
What caused those who lived in Lydda and Sharon to turn to the Lord?

_____

_____

Notice "all who lived" in those cities became Christians. We now have entire cities turning Christian at once.

There are two important points in these accounts. First, these encounters were miraculous and this obviously impressed onlookers. But second, they demonstrated conclusively that the gospel of Christ was not just a spiritual remedy. The good news was linked to material aspects of life. The Christian religion showed its true colors by dealing with every kind of need that troubled its hearers. We may not be impressed, but in that period this kind of good news had dramatic results because of the following perception...

Most of the Greek philosophers believed that body and spirit were separate. Physical things and the material world were evil and the spiritual realm was good. Later in church history this heresy was repeated in gnosticism. Separating the spirit from the body meant that most religions dealt only with afterlife or with some other spiritual reality. This made it easy for critics to doubt the incarnation and resurrection, since they thought Jesus was really only a spiritual being, perhaps inhabiting a man's body.

Because of this, sickness, political oppression, slavery, war and hunger were things people just lived with. But Christians suddenly claimed that Jesus came to deal with physical as well as spiritual matters. Paul delivered the slave girl in Acts 16:16-21 from economic slavery as well as from demons.

This ministry to the real pain that people felt in their immediate context is something we call wholistic ministry today. Acts is a ringing testimony of this proclamation of good news to the whole person.

3 — Check your note cards...can you find any other examples of wholistic ministry in Acts? Describe one situation:

_____

_____

_____

_____

APPLICATION

1 — Try this short exercise: think of a person you know in a different ethnic group who is not a Christian. Other than their need for Christ, list the needs or pain they might be feeling (unemployment, loneliness, hunger, etc.).

_____

_____

_____

_____

_____

2 — Read the section by Landrey starting on page 53 and "Ministry among Newcomers" by Hill starting on page 79.

When Landrey speaks of the ministry of service, what is he saying about the *style* of ministry?

_____

_____

_____

_____

Read the quote from the Lausanne Covenant and write a short summary of it:

_____

_____

_____

_____

Describe what "development" (Landrey, page 60) might include for an ethnic group living near your church:

_____

_____

_____

_____

Define what you think Hill means by "service evangelism" (page 82):

_____

_____

_____

_____

ACTION

1 — Take the needs you defined in question 1 under APPLICATION. Describe four things your church could do to meet these needs:

1) _____

2) _____

3) _____

4) _____

2 — If someone in your congregation was paying undocumented workers less than minimum wage, would this inequity fall under your definition of wholistic ministry? What could the church do in such a case?

_____

_____

_____

_____

3 — Choose an ethnic group living within two miles of your church.
If a large portion (or even a small number) of this group became
Christians — as in Lydda — how would the group change? What
values would change? Sketch out a vision of what you think they
might be like:

_____

_____

_____

_____

_____

_____

_____

_____

_____

_____

_____

_____

_____

_____

_____

_____

_____

Ethnic Ministry and People Groups

3

If you have never heard of the people group concept in evangelism or missions, here is a quick definition: people groups are those who see themselves as similar to certain others because of their language, cultural background, vocation or needs or for other reasons. They feel they have something in common with a group, and they tend to spend time with them. They are more relaxed with these people, communicate more easily with them than with anyone else, and tend to form most close relationships within .this group. A people group like this is usually limited somewhat by geography, but is primarily defined by the things the members share in common. People groups are important for us because the gospel will be heard and understood most quickly and most accurately if we can use this idea for communicating.

For example, if we wanted to reach Hispanics, it is not enough to say let's go preach to Spanish-speaking people. (It obviously hasn't worked in this country just to go preach to English-speaking people!) We need to define the people we want to present Christ to as completely as we can. It might be more helpful to identify Spanish-speaking, second-generation barrio gang members, living in East Los Angeles and attending a certain high school. This gives us a way to shape a gospel message more precisely. If we walked into a gang meeting in a three-piece suit, speaking English and handing out tracts, they might not listen very carefully. If we looked like them, thought like them, and especially if we showed our concern for them in concrete ways, they might be more open. We have to shape our message to fit who they are.

When Paul preached at the Areopagus (Acts 17:16-34), we might describe the group as generally male (though Damaris was there), well-educated, embracing certain philosophical beliefs (Epicurean and Stoic) and interested in religion. They were Greek-speaking (mainly Athenians, but some foreigners), probably known to each other because of regular discourse and because of "membership," not necessarily gainfully employed (probably wealthy if they could afford to stand around the Areopagus), and familiar with Greek poets.

Think about this description of the Areopagus bunch, and then read the sermon Paul preached to them. He looked around, knew exactly who he was talking to and talked right at them, and the Spirit did the rest. What if Paul had dragged out an old copy of

Stephen's sermon to the Sanhedrin? The Areopagus listeners would either have stoned him out of boredom, or slept through the whole talk.

REFLECTION

1 — Now read Acts 16:13-15

Paul was no dummy when it came to people group thinking. Describe the people group he found. How, specifically, do you think Paul shaped his message for this group? What new things did Christianity have to say to Philippian women which had never been said before? What needs do you think were present among them?

_____

_____

_____

_____

How could the gospel set a woman free in A.D. 40?

_____

_____

_____

_____

APPLICATION

1 — How can the gospel set free a Vietnamese woman, gathered at a downtown Seattle laundromat with her friends, in A.D. 1985? When was the last time you tried preaching to one? Don't worry if you haven't. For the time being, try to describe the characteristics of this people group:

_____

_____

_____

_____

2 — Try to use this way of looking at people groups to understand

another group in your city. Choose a group that lives within two miles of your church. Exhaustively describe them using every characteristic you can think of. Then try to understand what this means for evangelizing them. Especially think about their needs. How can you earn the credibility to be heard?

_____

_____

_____

_____

_____

_____

_____

3 — Using your note cards, check for any other people groups mentioned in Acts and describe their characteristics:

_____

_____

_____

_____

_____

_____

ACTION

1 — Take the work you did in question 2 above and go to the library to learn more about this people group. Try to find out what their needs are, how you can help. Find out if any other church is already helping them. Talk to one other person in your church about this group and share your findings. If you both feel excited about reaching out, talk to your pastor or someone else in leadership, and ask either if they have similar dreams.

Ethnic Ministry and Us

4

For some time now, as we have worked through these different aspects of ethnic ministry, we have completed a number of ACTION responses. This final study will help us to understand the big picture, *and* put the pieces together for our own ministry.

REFLECTION

Read Acts 2:5-12

At the very outset, the Holy Spirit caused the explosive beginning of the church right in the middle of an ethnic crowd. These people were all Jews, but Jews from "every nation under heaven." In Acts 1:8, Jesus himself lays out the scenario: "you will receive power when the Holy Spirit comes upon you; and you will be my witnesses in Jerusalem, and in all Judea and Samaria, and to the ends of the earth." In the first gasps of new life, the church faced "every nation under heaven" immediately outside the room where the Spirit fell. The people from "the ends of the earth" had already come to the doorstep of the church.

1 — Not only do we have a mandate to proclaim the gospel across cultural boundaries both at home and abroad, but we have this mandate communicated to us as emphatically as possible. Answer for yourself, in the space below, "what does this mean for me?" (Acts 2:12)

_____

_____

_____

_____

_____

2 — Read Acts 10:28, 34-35 What did God show Peter?

_____

_____

_____

_____

Rephrase Acts 10:34-35 in your own words:

_____

_____

_____

_____

_____

3 — Read Acts 15:1-35 Sketch out the issue in dispute in verse 1:

_____

_____

_____

_____

What was Peter's description of how a person could be saved:

_____

_____

_____

_____

The "men from Antioch" were called Judaizers. They wanted all Christians to look just like Jews. Have you ever known of a strong evangelistic group of Christians who wanted believers from another ethnic group to worship like them, dress like them, talk like them and start more churches just like theirs? In the early church, as now, this brings conflict. What was the judgment of the church elders?

_____

_____

_____

4

What do you think should be the basic values, practices or beliefs present in a new church within another ethnic group in your city? In other words, what basic message would you give to this church if you sat among the elders in Jerusalem?

_____

_____

_____

_____

_____

(What do you think your own church might think of the Haitian churches described by Bishop Golden on page 116? Ask yourself whether you or your friends might be prone to "judaizing" today!)

APPLICATION

1 — Read again Acts 1:8. It's interesting to treat Jerusalem, Judea and Samaria and the ends of the earth as three general categories of peoples for us to be witnesses to. We've talked about the ends of the earth, and especially how they have come to our own doorsteps. We've also talked about ministry to people, like Judeans and Samarians, who are close to us, either physically or culturally, but still different. Finally, we're faced with Jerusalem — our own people group. The gospel tells us of the balance we are to bring to ministry — our friends, our neighbors, the world — Jerusalem, Judea and Samaria, and the ends of the earth.

Ministering to our own people group makes good sense. If people group thinking is accurate, who can better share the gospel with people just like us, than us?

Read "Ministry Among American-born Chinese" by Dr. Law, starting on page 105.

Describe the characteristics Dr. Law notes that show how unique American-born Chinese are as a group:

_____

_____

_____

_____

_____

What things does the author suggest that might make the gospel more understandable by American-born Chinese?

_____

_____

_____

_____

_____

2 — Read "Ministry Among Internationals" by Stacy Bieler on page 99. This is cross-cultural ministry, and might be called "friendship evangelism." It has a lot to do with meeting something called "felt needs." In this case, loneliness can be a devastating problem for a student from another country, just arrived in the United States. List several of the suggestions the author recommends:

1) _____

2) _____

3) _____

4) _____

5) _____

6) _____

7) _____

8) _____

3 — It's helpful to know about some major things denominations are doing. This can be especially helpful when trading resources back and forth. Read "Ethnic Ministry Within the Churches" by Dr. DuBose, starting on page 65. Each denomination mentioned has resources for the ethnic groups listed in the article. Contact a local pastor from these denominations if you're looking for information or

4

write the Houston '85 committee at the address on the back of this book.

4 — Finally, read "When The World Arrives at Your Doorstep" by Rev. Westgate, starting on page 73. Take the transition stages listed, and decide whether your own church might fit in one of these stages. Then look around your city and select one church that could fit in each category. List the church and the category below:

5 — Take your note cards and find two churches in Acts experiencing the traumas of transition. Name and describe them:

ACTION

1 — If you have finished the study properly, you should have the following information at hand:

1. Characteristics of an ethnic people group
2. Needs description of an ethnic people group
3. Needs response for an ethnic people group
4. A vision statement for an ethnic people group
5. Two "action items" for the next month
6. An issue response for your church to a local problem

You now have almost everything you need to reach out in a sensitive and effective way. One understanding remains ... only the Spirit of God brings conviction, repentance and salvation. Your most important commitment must be to pray for these people. Whether they are from Jerusalem, Judea or Samaria, or from the ends of the earth, it is God's desire that "all nations under heaven" would turn to Christ. This effort will be immersed in prayer or it will never take place.

Begin to meet the needs of the people you believe God has led you to serve. Hold up the vision you have for these people and use this to pray. Always consider how God views these people and remember his delight at even one who comes into the kingdom.

Write us at the address on the back of this book if you are interested in participating in Houston '85. Pray for us and with us that Ethnic America will hear his voice!

Readings in
Ethnic Evangelism

The People of a New Ethnic America

C. Kirk Hadaway*

The history of America as a nation of immigrants has resulted in a society which can also be considered a nation of ethnics. We all came from somewhere else, even Native Americans, who crossed the land bridge from Siberia thousands of years ago. Most observers of American society would stop short of calling all Americans ethnics, however, because a dominant culture of sorts has emerged. This culture is most easily observed on television — in portrayal of the typical white, English-speaking, nominally Christian, well-educated family with 2.3 children.

The dominant culture of America is not strictly defined; it has blurred edges. And it also has its subcultures, such as the Deep South, or New England, where people consider themselves part of the dominant culture, but nevertheless possess a few additional cultural characteristics which make the region and its people quite different.

Ethnics are those who perceive themselves to be part of a culture other than the dominant culture, because of language, national origin or religious tradition. There is great variety in the ways an ethnic person retains characteristics. A Russian Jew in the Washington Heights area of Manhattan who speaks no English is obviously an ethnic, but what about the third-generation Chinese co-ed in Los Angeles who speaks no Chinese and has adopted a thoroughly Californian lifestyle? She may be considered an ethnic largely as a result of her own self-perception.

How Many Ethnics?

The 1980 census is by far the best instrument we have in deter-

* Dr. Kirk Hadaway is Director of Research for the Center for Urban Church Studies in Nashville, Tennessee, a program of the Southern Baptist Convention.

A Russian Jew who speaks no English is obviously an ethnic but what about the third-generation Chinese coed?

mining the ethnicity of America. All figures are actually estimates because the census did not account for undocumented residents and various discrepancies in definition for particular races. In 1980 the United States had the following racial/ethnic breakdown:

White (Non-Spanish)	79.6%
Black (Non-Spanish)	11.5%
Spanish Origin	6.4%
Asian/Pacific Islander	1.5%
American Indian/Eskimo/Aleut	.6%
Other	.4%

If we assume that all of the racial/ethnic categories other than non-Spanish whites are ethnics, we would conclude that the United States has 46.3 million ethnics, or 20.4 percent of its population. We know, however, that this figure is low because many of the white non-Spanish persons are also ethnics. If we adjust the figures to account for them and for some four million undocumented ethnics who were missed in the 1980 census, the new total is 81.5 million ethnics, or 36 percent of the U.S. population.

Trends Since 1970

There is a widespread awareness that the ethnicity of America has increased since 1970. This perception is accurate. The ethnic population has surged due to immigration from Asia, refugees from Cuba and other parts of the world, and large numbers of documented and undocumented persons from Mexico, Latin American countries and Haiti.

It is difficult to estimate the total ethnic population in 1970 in order to make a comparison, but is possible to look at the increase in three groups: Hispanics, Asians and native Americans.

Hispanics

The Hispanic population has grown enormously in the United States over the past ten years. In 1980 the census counted 14.6 million persons of Spanish origin, up from 9.1 million in 1970 (a gain of 5.5 million, or 61 percent). This increase has been fueled by two factors: high fertility and increased immigration (both legal and illegal).

If we go back even further to 1950, the growth of the Hispanic population is even more dramatic, increasing from four million to its present 14.6 million, a 265 percent increase. This rapid rate of growth, when compared to the much slower growth of the nation at large, has meant that the percent of the nation that is Hispanic has been steadily increasing.

Year	Total U.S. Population	Hispanics	Percentage of U.S. Population
1950	151.3	4.0	2.7%
1960	179.3	6.9	3.9%
1970	203.2	10.5	5.2%
1980	226.5	14.6	6.4%

(Note: all figures in millions)

Incorporated in the definition of Hispanic are several subgroups:

Mexican-American	59.8%
Puerto Rican	13.8%
Cuban-American	5.5%
Other Hispanic	20.9%

All of the Hispanic groups have been growing in recent years, but the increase has been larger among Puerto Ricans, Cubans and "other Hispanics." Mexican-Americans constituted 70 percent of the Hispanic population in 1950, a figure that has been reduced to 60 percent in 1980.

Growth in the Hispanic population can be attributed to two factors — fertility and immigration. Two-thirds of the growth stems from the high fertility rate among Hispanic women. Recent statistics show that the fertility rate is around 59 percent higher for Hispanic women when compared to non-Hispanic women. Also, a larger proportion of Hispanics are in their child-bearing years, or are younger — a sure sign of growth momentum for the future.

Latin Americans have made up an ever-increasing share of the immigrant population since 1968. Before that year they were only 15 percent of the *legal* total. From 1968 to present, Latin Americans have averaged 40 percent of the legal immigrants. This increase was largely due to changes in legal restrictions to immigration.

Even though the Immigration and Nationality Act of 1965 (which went into effect in 1968) made it easier for Latin Americans to emigrate to the United States, other changes made the process more lengthy and cut off a program which allowed over 400,000 temporary Mexican workers annually to enter the United States. This cutoff, when coupled with the high Mexican birth rate, unemployment at extremely high levels, and a severe per capita income differential between the United States and Mexico ($12,530 vs $2,063 in 1981), stimulated the heavy illegal immigration that continues today. Estimates of the total illegal immigration to the United States range from 100,000 to 500,000 persons annually. Around 50 to 60 percent of these illegal entrants are Mexicans.

Asians

The Immigration Act of 1965 dramatically increased the number of Asians eligible to enter the United States. By 1979 Asians accounted for 39 percent of the legal immigration to the United States. This new policy, when combined with the addition of over 400,000 Southeast Asian refugees, raised the total number of Asians in the U.S. from 1.5 million in 1970 to 3.5 million in 1980, a gain of nearly 150 percent.

Many different Asian groups are represented in the total, with Chinese, Filipino and Japanese being the largest. All of the groups have grown since 1970.

	1970	1980	Change
Chinese	431,583	812,178	98%
Filipino	336,731	781,894	132%
Japanese	588,324	715,331	22%
Korean	69,510	357,390	414%

In addition, there were 387,000 Asian Indians, 245,000 Vietnamese, 48,000 Laotians and 45,000 Thai in 1980.

American Indians

The American Indian population increased between 1970 and 1980. Obviously, none of this came through immigration, and much was not due to birthrate. Instead, the Census Bureau improved counting procedures for Indians and produced a more accurate figure than in 1970.

California has the largest numbers of American Indians, followed by Oklahoma, Arizona, New Mexico and North Carolina. In fact, one-half of the native American population lived in these five states.

New Mexico had the highest percentage of its population classified as native American (8 percent), followed by South Dakota (6.5 percent).

Eskimos and Aleuts are not included in these figures, but numbered 42,149 and 14,177 respectively, living for the most part in Alaska.

Urban Ethnics

Hispanics are a highly urban population. In 1980, 88 percent lived in metropolitan areas. Los Angeles has 2 million Hispanics and New York City has 1.5 million. Los Angeles is larger than any Central American country in terms of its Hispanic population.

Cuban-Americans are more concentrated in metro areas than any other Hispanic group. Virtually 100 percent live in urban areas, with over half in the Miami metropolitan area.

Mexican Americans are more dispersed, with one-fifth found in

Los Angeles, and other large groups in Chicago, San Antonio, Houston and other "Sun-belt" cities. In San Antonio, Mexican-Americans form the majority and have the first Mexican-American Mayor (Henry Cisneros) in the nation.

In New York City, Puerto Ricans are the most dominant Hispanic group, with 43 percent of the mainland population.

Like Hispanics, Asians and Pacific Islanders are highly urbanized. Over 90 percent live in metropolitan areas.

Over half of all native Americans live in cities, surprising because of our expectation that Indians generally reside on rural reservations.

Ethnic Ministry in Cities

Raymond Bakke*

The Good News is not only that Jesus shed his blood for the world, but also that he got his blood from the world. That is good news especially in a racist society, in a world of yellow, black and brown people.

The opening paragraph of the New Testament lists the lineage of Christ and confirms his mixed heritage. In that list of names are four women. They could be called the other women in the family of Jesus, or skeletons in the closet. They are Tamar, Rahab, Ruth and Bathsheba.

The story of Tamar chronicles the unfortunate circumstances of the three sons of Judah, two of whom married Tamar. A very sexually explicit story, rather delicately told. But the bottom line is that Tamar produced twins by her own father-in-law, who became ancestors of Jesus.

The story of Rahab is really of the same genre. Rahab ran a brothel in Jericho. Where, after all, would the spies hide where the lights are low and people don't ask your name? She lied, put the Gestapo on a false trail and then said, "I want to believe in your God."

Ruth was a Moabite woman, married and widowed. In her story, it was the dark ages of Israel, and the whole Moabitic culture had its roots in Lot, who was made drunk by his daughters. He retaliated by impregnating them — Moab was one of the results. Out of an incestuous culture, a child became an ancestor of Jesus.

The fourth story is of Bathsheba, the wife of David's trusted soldier. Bathsheba, along with David, was involved in an adulterous

---

* Dr. Ray Bakke is an experienced urban pastor, and faculty member at Northern Baptist Seminary.

affair and later a cover-up.

Martin Luther was the first one to examine this text and notice that all four women are foreigners. Luther said that Tamar and Rahab were Canaanites; Ruth a Moabite and Bathsheba was presumably a Hittite. Luther concluded that the passage is about mission.

Raymond Brown, a contemporary scholar, has looked at the passage and said that Matthew may have chosen them because they all had unusual birth stories, and perhaps they were chosen to be a historical support group for Mary, who was having a little difficulty explaining where her child came from.

That Jesus choreographs in his body, in his own ethnic family history, the ethnicity of the Middle East, can have meaning for us in our day. The opening paragraph of the New Testament says Jesus was *mestizo,* and almost everybody in South America is mestizo. They can hear this with joy and know that they are also made in the image of God.

What we in America consider to be minorities are in reality the global majority. There are about 4.7 billion people in the world today. In 16 years, the population of Asia alone will be over 4 billion. Every few seconds, 100 babies or so are born in the world. Forty-nine are yellow, 13 white and the rest are black and brown. That means that Caucasians are 13 percent of those being born in the world. We are the minority, and it's time we begin to realize it. Most of the world is not white. That has profound implications for Americans.

There is no denying it is so. The numbers are all too clear. First, there is what is called the Asianization of the world. This is not just one culture, but many, with many different languages, customs and religions. The integration of Asians into the religious mainstream has been successful. There were only two Presbyterian Korean churches in Chicago in 1966, but 42 in 1976 and over 100 today.

The Hispanics are impacting our country as significantly. The Mexican-American population of the Los Angeles basin totals 4 1/2 million. The United States is the fourth largest Spanish nation in the world. Unfortunately, the evangelization of these people has been less successful than that of the Asians. There isn't a single capital in all of South America that has fewer evangelicals per capita than greater Los Angeles.

The United States is the second largest Polish nation, and the largest Jewish nation.

This situation is not unique to the United States. Three years ago there was a riot on a subway with Pakistanis and people from India rioting while Nigerians watched in utter amazement. This happened in London, chief city of one of the largest empires the world has seen. Now the world is coming to London.

There are communities in Amsterdam that are nearly one-fifth Moluccan, Malaysian, Indonesian or Surinamese. Thirteen percent of Paris is Algerian, because of the 300,000 Algerian refugees living there. Hundreds of thousands of Turks live in cities in Germany. One million Japanese live in Sao Paulo, Brazil, the largest Japanese colony outside of Japan.

Where are all these people migrating to? The answer is the cities. And it's happening very quickly. We are producing two Chicagos a month on this planet. In other words, the new growth of people in the world (birth rate minus death rate) amounts to enough people to fill up two cities the size of Chicago every month.

The United States is no exception. In a Yale study, historians reported that more people have come north to cities in this century than went west to farms in the last century.

Identification with cities is not unique to our era. Ezekiel 16 is a key passage that indicates God's perspective on cities. Starting in verse 45 it says, "Your mother was a Hittite, your father an Amorite, and your elder sister is Samaria who lived in the north with her daughters, and your younger sister is Sodom who lived in the south with her daughters."

In the Bible there is a theology of place. In other words, in the Bible, peoples become places, and there is no distinction. That is what Old Testament scholars call "corporate solidarity motifs," someone always being in a family context, from some place — Simon Bar Jonah, Saul of Tarsus, etc.

Cities are also connected to each other. There is no such biblical place as away. You cannot distinguish the migration of ethnics apart from the places they represent.

What, then, is the strategy for reaching this microcosm of the human family? It is important to differentiate between a ministry of ethnics versus a ministry to ethnics. The latter is very paternalistic.

It is not a matter of determining what we are going to do to them, but rather deciding what God is calling them to do.

There are some strategies that can aid in effective ministry of ethnics. The white fright that leads to white flight is an important barrier to overcome. The best way to do that is to change the perspective of many citizens. If they can see themselves as stewards

More people have come north to cities in this century than went west to farms in the last century

of the richest country in the world, both in terms of resources and opportunities, then perhaps they can catch the vision of acceptance and evangelization. Otherwise, they will retreat to a simple civil religion and lose the cutting edge of the ministry.

Second, we need to change our concept of missions, especially of the tradition of furloughs — not the kind where missionaries from Buenos Aires come home to Chicago to tell what they're doing and take an offering for Buenos Aires. But a furlough where the missionary from Buenos Aires comes to Chicago and teaches us cross-cultural skills while we upgrade the ministry tool kit of the missionary and expose the missionary to what God is doing in the city so he or she can go back to Buenos Aires and do some of the same things.

We need that two-way brokering of resources; foreign missions agencies and their home missions counterparts should travel a two-way street. We have understood missions in this country as mainly overseas; because of this we are writing off huge sections of the ethnic ministry in the city.

We can take a different approach to the resources on the home front, also. What a helpful thing it would be to inventory the denominational resource persons with access to cross-cultural skills. The computer age, a desire to reach beyond denominational bounds and attempts at networking can all make that possible. By giving our skills and talents to other members of the body, we could easily set up task forces to deal with the unique opportunities in Miami, Los Angeles, Detroit and other major areas.

Wholeness in Ministry

J. Paul Landrey*

"But Jesus called them to Himself, and said, You know that the rulers of the Gentiles lord it over them, and their great men exercise authority over them. It is not so among you, but whoever wishes to become great among you shall be your servant, and whoever wishes to be first among you shall be your slave; just as the Son of Man did not come to be served, but to serve, and to give His life a ransom for many." (Matthew 20:25-28)

Jesus' words and his works constituted a single ministry (a whole). His works were signs of the Kingdom he was announcing and describing in his words. When he saw the crowds he had compassion on them because they were harassed and helpless "like sheep without a shepherd" (Matt. 9:36). He saw, he felt and he acted.

He never made a distinction between the verbal announcement and compassionate works which so many do today. In those brief years in which he ministered there was a wholeness to what he said and did. They were intrinsically related, the one to the other. They flowed in an ever increasing crescendo of activity from a Single Source for a singular purpose. He himself said that it was the Father who was responsible for both his words and his works:

Truly, truly, I say to you, the Son can do nothing of Himself, unless it is something He sees the Father doing; for whatever

* Rev. Paul Landrey is Director of World Vision's U.S. Ministry Division and served as an urban missionary to Bogota, Colombia and Sao Paulo, Brazil.

the Father does, these things the Son also does in like manner (John 5:19b).

... I can do nothing on my own initiative, as I hear, I judge ... (John 5:30a).

... My teaching is not mine, but his who sent me (John 7:16).

It is therefore wrong to dichotomize the gospel into evangelism and social action, separating the verbal announcement from concrete, compassionate works. As Richard Dickenson says:

> The issue of development is not something peripheral or extraneous to the theology and spiritual life of the church and Christians, but something which pushes them into the very core of the gospel itself. Inadequate involvement in it is not only a moral problem, but a theological problem.

Social action is integral to the mission of evangelism. As Jesus went about doing good (such as healing the sick and feeding the hungry) and preaching the Kingdom, he did not label one as spiritual and the other as temporal. There was no establishing priorities or polarizing them. All his words and works were essential to his ministry to humankind's total well-being. If the church is true to its calling it will emulate the ministry of Christ when he was here on earth. Like his, our ministry is to be a full-orbed and concrete expression of love and service to persons.

Our ministry can be broken down into three important areas:

MINISTRY IS SERVICE

In the Matthew 20 passage quoted above, we read how Jesus handled the quest for privilege among the disciples. The mother of the two sons of Zebedee came to Jesus asking for privileges for her sons. His reply was that they had no right to expect particular positions in the Kingdom. The disciples were angry with the two brothers.

Jesus called them together for that important message on power and authority. "If one of you wants to be great, he must be a servant of the rest ... like the Son of Man who did not come to be served, but to serve and give his life as a ransom for many."

He literally took the typical understanding of power and inverted it. In a word, he turned the organization chart upside down. He focused attention upon the heart motivation and not upon outward appearances, by reminding them how he had come and served. This makes the words of John 20:21 all the more important: "As the Father has sent me into the world, so send I you." He seems to be saying that we are to go in the same manner, for the same reason, and with the same authority to accomplish his purposes.

Ministry in a biblical sense is synonymous with service. A servant is one who serves another entirely out of his own will and desire. Joshua, as a young person, ministered to Moses, though in rank he was a prince of the tribe of Ephraim. Priests and Levites in the Old Testament offered services to God on behalf of the people and to the people. Paul, a leader among Jews, ministered the gospel to the Gentiles (considered non-people by the Jews). Jonathan, son of Israel's first king, ministered to David long before David was chosen as Saul's successor.

A person who ministers or serves is seen as one who is subservient to a master. In our case we are servants of the Master, the Lord Jesus Christ who has been given all authority in heaven and earth. The love of God (agape love) fully expressed itself in service. "God was in Christ reconciling the world to himself." He gave everything for those who deserve nothing.

Jesus also demonstrated that we must begin by serving the people closest to us. Washing the feet of the disciples in the upper room was a dramatic object lesson for them and for us. While the disciples must have been wondering among themselves, "Where is the servant to wash our feet?" Jesus simply went about the task of doing what needed to be done. That image of the serving Lord Jesus with a towel and basin should be indelibly burned into our hearts and minds.

The Thailand Statement says:

> We are also the servants of Jesus Christ who is himself both "the servant" and "the Lord." He calls us, therefore, not only to obey him as Lord in every area of our lives, but also to serve as he served. We confess that we have not suffi-

ciently followed his example of love in identifying with the poor and hungry, the deprived and the oppressed. Yet all God's people "should share his concern for justice and reconciliation throughout human society and for the liberation of (people) from every kind of oppression."

(Lausanne Covenant, paragraph 5).

The Lausanne Covenant also declares that "in the church's mission of sacrificial service, evangelism is primary" (paragraph 6). This is not to deny that evangelism and social action are integrally related, but rather to acknowledge that of all the tragic needs of human beings none is greater than alienation from their Creator and the terrible reality of eternal death for those who refuse to repent and believe. If therefore we do not commit ourselves with urgency to the task of evangelization, we are guilty of an inexcusable lack of human compassion.

MINISTRY IS IDENTIFICATION

Ministry only occurs when we act in love. "This is what love is: it is not that we have loved God but that he loved us and sent his son to be the means by which our sins are forgiven" (John 4:10). The model Jesus gives us is one of complete abandonment of rights to power, prestige, possessions and privilege. His focus was to incarnate himself with the powerless, the outcast and the lowly, without identifying with any of the prevailing political structures of the Greeks, Romans, Jews or Zealots. The other thing that really mattered was that people found "the pearl of great price," that is, fullness in Christ in the Kingdom of God.

"This is how we know what love is: Christ gave his life for us. We too, then, ought to give our lives for our brothers! If a rich person sees his brother in need, yet closes his heart against his brother, how can we claim he loves God? My children, our love should not be just words and talk; it must be true love which shows itself in action" (I John 3:16-18). What Jesus said and did, he wants us to say and do.

It is possible for us to identify from a distance without becoming incarnate or involved in a world which so desperately needs the ministry of the Kingdom. It is integral involvement, however, that overcomes the barriers to ministry. A Brazilian church leader has said:

> We are working today not from the world but with the world. This distinction is very important because we used to bring solutions to the people — schools, hospitals, churches, very beautiful churches. Now the important thing for us is to discover solutions together with the people. We need to begin by proving to them that we are all human beings — not animals and objects, but men and women, children of God. The real foreigners in Brazil are the native-born Brazilians who have no concern for great human need. There are many people working with us who were born outside of Brazil ... you are not foreigners, no, because you come here with the great decision to understand our people, not only our language, but our psychology and our problems.
>
> You are here to assume our problems. This is what I call incarnation because the Son of God always being the Son of God is here assuming our problems. You are not foreigners, you are brothers and sisters.

We don't hear enough about the Kingdom of God in evangelical circles today. Yet this was the prime theme on Jesus' lips and the total absorption of his life. He refers to it over one hundred times.

Unfortunately, we live in a world in which half the people have no vital relationship with Jesus Christ. They do not participate in the peace, justice and community that the Kingdom of God brings. That would be bad enough. The other half of the world possess more than they need and don't share it adequately. Increasingly they prevent those who have little from any participation or control over their own destiny. Unfortunately the majority of these are so-called "Christian nations."

This has provoked anger and a great deal of mistrust in the rest of the world. Perhaps this is why Paul Hiebert of Fuller Theological Seminary indicates that missions will become more involved in development in the next ten years, and only those who do so will be permitted to function in much of the non-Western world.

MINISTRY IS WHOLENESS

In Luke 4:18-19 we read, "The spirit of the Lord is upon me because he has chosen me to bring good news to the poor. He has sent me to proclaim liberty to the captives and recovering of sight to the blind; to set free the oppressed and announce that the time has come when the Lord will save his people."

In this presentation in the synagogue of Nazareth, Jesus quotes from Isaiah 61:1,2. The context in the Old Testament is not spiritual, but physical. In a sense what Jesus is doing is declaring the ministry he is about to embark upon. It includes several areas of special concern:

Good News to the Poor — The economically disinherited.
What would be good news to the poor? To make them content in their poverty? To offer them a reward in the hereafter? The good news they need to hear is that there is adequacy within the Kingdom of God and the relationships which it requires. Poverty is not God's will, it is ours by default.

Liberty to the Captives — The socially and politically disinherited.
This refers to the total captivity of persons, both spiritual and physical. People exploit other people and use them for their own ends. The Kingdom would stop all exploitation and make people an end in themselves as the children of God. The foundation of the Kingdom is that we should be in bondage to no person but be bondslaves only to Jesus Christ.

Recovering of Sight to the Blind — The physically disinherited.
The Kingdom of God stands for life at its fullest. Sin, error, disease and death are anti-life, so the Kingdom challenges them. Healing is part of the redemptive purpose of God, not a bait for evangelism. It stands in its own right as a part of the coming of the Kingdom. The healing of relationships, the healing of nations, the healing of hurts and diseases are included.

The Setting Free of the Oppressed — The morally and spiritually disinherited.

Another translation of this passage reads, "to strengthen with forgiveness them that are bruised." Bruises that need forgiveness to be banished must be moral and spiritual bruises. Ours is a world of moral consequences. We bruise ourselves upon the moral facts of the universe. We do not break God's laws, they break us.

The only thing that can take away those moral bruises is forgiveness and we have been given the ministry of reconciliation. The Kingdom offers a new birth — a fresh start. As Jesus said, "Unless you are born again you cannot see the Kingdom of God." This is the evangelistic thrust which calls all people to recognize their alienation from God, their sinfulness and their need for a Savior. This Savior is the King and by acceptance of his sacrifice, they become born by grace into his Kingdom.

The Time When the Lord Will Save His People — The Lord's Year of Jubilee.

This refers to the Jewish Year of Jubilee when every 50 years there was new national beginning. All debts were cancelled, all slaves were freed and all land was redistributed.

The dynamic of this structured equality was to bring a closer fellowship and a recognition that God was the owner of all things. People could not own land — it belonged to God; they owned the produce to the extent that they were willing to work for it. The Jewish Year of Jubilee worked from the social order to the individual. Jesus took the concept and enlarged it.

The Christian can work from both directions, from the individual to the social order and from the social order to the individual. Unfortunately, the Jews did not seriously follow God's pattern. "What he requires of us is this: to do what is best, to show constant love, and to live in humble fellowship with our God" (Micah 6:8).

The Spirit of the Lord Is Upon Me

The dynamic thrust for the whole program of the Kingdom depends upon the flow and power of the Spirit of God. The method of bringing in this new Kingdom must be consistent with his Spirit. This rules out for the Christian the methods and authority of natural power. If we should bring in the Kingdom of God by compulsion, then it would not be the Kingdom — it would be something else. The Holy Spirit works through the people of God in the same way today as he did in New Testament times. As the Lord explained in John 14 and 16, the Holy Spirit glorifies the Son. In modern day terminology the Holy Spirit contextualizes the lordship of Jesus Christ.

SUGGESTIONS FOR A MINISTRY OF WHOLENESS

There are several ways in which the church can play a unique role. First, the Christian is uniquely motivated by the Holy Spirit to serve people Christ has sent us with a ministry which reflects his own — fulfilling both the Great Commission and the Great Commandment. We are both to go and make disciples of all nations and to love God with all our hearts and our neighbor as ourselves as Christ did, incarnate among persons. The best humanists cannot match the Christian in depth of motivation to serve, nor do they have the enablement of the living Christ.

The Indian theologian, Amalorpavadass, notes:

> As long as Christians are, or appear to be, outsiders and foreigners, a marginal group or a pressure group, not integrated into the community, just so long, they have not even started their mission. Nor are they fit for it. Nor do they have the authentic spirit of the church. Christ's way is that everything is done from within.

Second, for Christians the goal of development is distinctive. The Christian church dare not limit development to mere economic growth or individual progress. We must be wary of making Western-style comfort and security our aim because we have a higher purpose. We should see the goal as persons "in community made whole in Christ." Amalorpavadass adds that "salvation or integral development is the total liberation of man from sin and all its forces and consequences so that man may be more a man."

Without spiritual redemption there is no development, only a patching of old wineskins. Experience shows that people who benefit from technological innovations and better health often use their gains to their personal advantage only. Increased income may only go to purchase new stereos or bigger houses.

Christians, indeed, may be the only ones capable of the radical change in values that would foster an appropriate and just use of new resources. John Perkins observes that Christians can uniquely contribute to and benefit from community development "because they make the necessary break with the present system and its mindset through repentance."

Finally, Christians can avoid the paternalism and cultural imperialism that usually accompany secular efforts in development — either national or international. Missions, unfortunately, have a spotted record in this regard. Christians today should recognize the image of God in every person and culture.

There is no one ideal culture that expresses all the diversity that people can create. God delights in the variety of lifeways that he ordained. Even the folkways of the poorest of the poor, imbued with common grace, have worth and beauty. Sin is also manifest in every culture, in different expressions. Ours is certainly no exception. Recognizing this, we should not be prone to judge others and set up ourselves and our own technology as examples. Rather we must be open to learn humbly from others, being vulnerable, as well as to teach and to lead.

Here are several illustrations that emphasize the importance of looking closely at why we do what we do. We need to understand the role our own philosophy or ideology plays in all we do.

A highly respected leader of the Colombian church was reviewing an animal loan project with his North American evangelical colleague. The project was designed to help families improve their diet and build economic independence. Starter animals were given to a few families and gradually the stewardship/ownership plan was extended to additional families as the new animals were born, yet the Colombian was uneasy. "We can't do it this way," he finally announced. "Why not?" asked the startled missionary. "Because they're making a profit." "But that's what we want, don't we?" "No, we are brothers, not capitalists."

In South Africa the government, in pursuit of its apartheid policies, forcibly cleared a city slum of Black inhabitants in order to force them back to their homelands. They approached the neighboring Anglican church for help. Had the church supported apartheid, it would not have given the Black South Africans sanctuary in its own compound, which it proceeded to do. The church consciously opposed the ideology of the government and identified with the people who were being unjustly treated.

SUMMARY

If the church is to resemble Christ's ministry in word and work, personal attitudes may need to change. The Thailand Statement emphasized the following four:

> The first is love ... We have had to repent of prejudice, disrespect and even hostility towards the very people we want to reach for Christ. We have also resolved to love others as God in Christ has loved us, and to identify with them in their situation as he identified himself with us in ours.
>
> Secondly, humility ... Other people's resistance to the gospel has sometimes been our fault. Imperialism, slavery, religious persecution in the name of Christ, racial pride and prejudice (whether anti-black, anti-white, anti-jewish, anti- arab or any other kind), cultural insensitivity, and indifference to the plight of the needy and the powerless — these are some of the evils which have marred the church's testimony and put stumbling blocks in other people's road to faith. We resolve in future to spread the gospel with greater humility.
>
> Thirdly, integrity ... The character and conduct of the message-bearer. Our witness loses credibility when we contradict it by our life or life-style. Our light will shine only when others can see our good works (Matt. 5:16). In a word, if we are to speak of Jesus with integrity, we have to resemble him.
>
> The fourth emphasis has to do with power. We know that we are engaged in a spiritual battle with demonic forces. Evangelism often involves a power encounter, and in conversion Jesus Christ demonstrates that he is stronger than the strongest principalities and powers of evil by liberating their victims. Strategy and organization are not enough; we need to

pray earnestly for the power of the Holy Spirit. God
has not given us a spirit of fear, but of boldness.

Service means voluntarily giving up everything for others, serving
those closest to us and allowing them to serve us, assuming the problems of others (incarnation), giving in a context of self-sacrifice, being
radical in contrast to the systems of this world, living as an obedient
disciple of the Lord, and recognizing that servant love is more powerful
than any human authority. It breaks through cultural, religious, historical, geographical and racial barriers. Jesus' life proclaimed the
Kingdom of God. His words and works constituted a single ministry (a
whole). He asks his Body to say and do the same today.

Ethnic Ministry Within the Churches

Francis DuBose*
Daniel Sanchez

One of the most significant developments in the American Protestant denominations since mid-century has been the growing presence of ethnics within their ranks. The impact of this ethnic presence in the traditional churches has been phenomenal over the last two decades. It has not only brought new life and vitality, it has brought a new sense of identity and direction to the traditionally European (and strongly Anglo) rooted denominations.

The purpose of this study is to focus on this striking phenomenon. Because it will be impossible to survey all of the denominations, we shall look at four mainline groups. Although the limitation of space prevents an in-depth look at any one group, the following groups are representative and the activities described will be typical.

The United Methodist Church

With deep roots in the Anglo tradition of Britain and America, United Methodism now sees itself as "a faith community enriched by the diverse heritage of its people. They are of many histories and cultures — Black, White, Asian American, Hispanic and Native American — but one in Christ."

Methodists witnessed the emergence of separate Black denominations growing out of a special social history. Recent decades, however, have witnessed not only Blacks becoming a growing part of American Methodism but the ethnic-language groups as well. An indication of the seriousness with which United Methodists have accepted this

*Professor DuBose teaches at Golden Gate Theological Seminary in San Francisco, and is an astute observer and analyst of America's ethnic scene. Professor Sanchez is on the faculty at Southwestern Theological Seminary in Dallas and is a former missionary in Central America.

challenge is demonstrated in the priorities which they have established in their present agenda.

In 1980, the General Conference established "Developing and Strengthening the Ethnic Minority Local Church" as its "number one" priority for 1981-84. The directions were made clear:

> By speaking of the ethnic minority local churches it will be understood such churches are "composed primarily of Blacks, Hispanics, Native American, and Pacific and Asian Americans — persons with a history of being exploited, oppressed and neglected, but who have a rich heritage of culture, lifestyle and theological insight." ("Emerging Directions Document," General Council Ministries, United Methodist Church, 1978.)

The strategy for this new program was developed with seven major guidelines, and specific directives were developed for each of the four major guidelines of ministry: (1) Evangelism and Church Growth; (2) Nurture; (3) Worship; (4) Outreach; (5) Ministries; (6) Organization; (7) Church Development and Buildings. To implement this priority program, $5 million was appropriated for each year. The General Council of Ministries, through the Ethnic Minority Coordinating Committee, was given the administrative responsibility for the program.

United Methodists were so inspired by this program that the 1984 General Conference set as its 1985-88 Missional Priority to continue "Developing and Strengthening the Ethnic Minority Local Church." An example of how this is being implemented in a given locality may be seen in the California-Nevada Conference which covers Northern California and part of Nevada. There are in this Conference 47 ethnic churches: 6 Chinese, 5 Filipino, 14 Japanese, 6 Korean, 1 Taiwanese, 8 Black, 5 Hispanic, and 2 Native American. In addition, there are 23 ethnic minority fellowships. The goal is to have ethnic congregations constitute 25 percent of the total congregations in the Conference.

In addition to Evangelism and Church Growth, Methodists are making ethnic self-determination, Anglo attitudes, social justice, and other issues vital to the concern of ethnics, essential aspects of a holistic ministry.

The Lutheran Church of America

The modern interest of the Lutheran Church of America in ethnic minorities has its antecedent in a 1964 statement on Race Relations in response to the Civil Rights Act of that year. The 1974 Convention of LCA commissioned an investigation regarding the status of minorities in the church and called for a long-range project to set goals for the rest of the decade ending on the twentieth anniversary of the statement on Race Relations. Two years later, in 1976, the statement was presented, calling for a six-year program: "Goals and Plans for Minority Ministry 1978-1984." The first three aspects of the program which was approved can be found in appendix I.

The other three aspects which expressed similar concerns and projected comparable goals were: Cooperate with Other Communities of Faith; Develop Professional Leadership; Support the Organization.

The first year of the new program, 1979-1980, gains in membership were experienced among all minority groups: American Indian, from 1,700 to 6,198; Hispanic, from 8,894 to 10,151. In 1980, one new Black, two new Hispanic and four new Asian congregations were started.

In 1981 two new Hispanic and three new Black congregations were begun. In 1980 there was special support for 77 congregations in racially transitional and poverty communities, and in 1981 there was special support for 106 such congregations.

In terms of leadership training and participation, gains have been made at most levels. In 1981, there were 29 Asian pastors, 49 Black pastors, 42 Hispanic pastors and 5 Native American pastors. In the academic year of 1981-82, there were 20 minority students out of 503 in LCA seminaries. In 1981, there were 17 minority persons serving predominantly white congregations. In colleges full-time minority faculty increased from 32 to 45 from 1980 to 1981. In the same period in the Social Services Agencies, full-time Executive-Administrative Minority Personnel increased from 58 to 100, and Professional Minority Staff increased from 340 to 606. From these records, it is apparent that the Lutheran Church of America is serious about the implications of its goals for minority ministry, from attitudes to congregational development to leadership sharing.

The United Presbyterian Church

In modern times there has been a deepening of conviction and a growing involvement in the struggles of ethnic minorities in the United Presbyterian Church. Two examples which reflect this are: "A Comprehensive Strategy on Racial Justice in the 1980s for the Presbyterian Church (U.S.A.)," and "The Fund for Legal Aid for Racial and Intercultural Justice."

A major arm of the Presbyterian Church is the National Asian Presbyterian Council. It was formed in 1972 and publishes a monthly periodical called CelebrASIAN. It is a platform for the expression of the various Asian voices in the denomination such as the National Chinese, Japanese, and Philippine Presbyterian Conferences. To enhance the witness at the local level, the denomination has developed the "Major Mission Find" for training programs in evangelism for racial/ethnic groups to enhance congregational development.

In November 1979, a significant event took place with major implications for Presbyterian Hispanic ministry. It was "The Hispanic Symposium." Its purpose was "to study, to analyze, and to reflect upon the Presbyterian presence among Hispanics; and to provide new directions for ministries among Hispanics in the Southwest." One recommendation led to the creation of the "consulting Committee on Hispanic Minorities in the Southwest." Some of the major areas of concern relate to such basic matters as evangelism, stewardship, and Christian education. In addition, attention was directed toward urban mission, border ministries, youth work, the empowerment of Hispanic women, the aging, congregational development, physical facilities of churches, and professional development. Behind it all was a strong affirmation of the Hispanic culture and a determination to give the Hispanic churches an opportunity for full participation in denominational life.

The oldest and one of the strongest ethnic ministries among Presbyterians is with Native Americans. The work was begun in 1742 on Long Island, New York. Work began among Pima Indians of Arizona in 1870.

Today there are over 100 Native American congregations in the UPC. The Dakota Presbytery is a totally Indian judicatory. The Cook Christian Training School of Tempe, Arizona has a program of continuing education for Native American pastors and laity with some 300 enrolled.

The Native American Church Development Association leads in undergirding ministry to the churches and the Native American community. Other agencies seek to inform the congregations in general concerning Native American ministry. The denomination has also been active in various Native American causes. For example, it provided significant aid in funding the United Tribes of North Dakota Development Corporation.

Besides the minority persons, men and women, who serve at various levels of leadership in the denominational structure, the UPC has been especially sensitive to create positions where there is now adequate minority input into the various program agencies of the denomination.

The Southern Baptist Convention

Southern Baptists, the most culturally diversified Protestant denomination in America, worship and study the Bible in more than 87 languages and dialects. More than 4,600 language-culture congregations, with nearly 250,000 members are affiliated with the Southern Baptist Convention. These congregations represent 84 of the nation's 500 ethnic groups and 97 tribes and sub-tribes of the 495 American Indian tribes. In addition to this, the Convention has ministeries to international seamen in more than 30 port cities; 839 congregations and/or departments of deaf persons, and a ministry to internationals which includes 406 participating churches and ministries in the United Nations as well as among diplomats in the nation's capitol.

Perhaps the greatest contributing factor to the success of Southern Baptist ethnic work has been the sensitivity of its leaders to socio-cultural trends among ethnic groups. Under the leadership of Dr. Oscar Romo, the Language Missions Division of the Baptist Home Mission Board has preached and practiced an indigenous philosophy. This philosophy gives top priority to the planting of ethnic congregations. During the past 10 years an average of 245 ethnic congregations have been established; their objective is to have 6,210 new congregations by the year 2000.

A method that has been used to establish new ethnic congregations is known as the "Laser Church Growth Thrust." This consists of a group of well-trained persons going to a city and working with local leaders to survey and contact persons of a specific ethnic group. Generally by the end of two weeks this group has contacted enough persons to get a Bible study fellowship going. One such group worked with First Chinese Baptist Church in Phoenix, Arizona to survey the northern part of the city in 1983. Today the new congregation is averaging more than 100 in worship. This congregation is made up primarily of American-born, young, professional Chinese persons who worship in English with some usage of Mandarin.

The quickness with which Southern Baptists have responded to the opportunity to minister to refugees has contributed to the establishment of ethnic congregations. The influx of Cubans in the early sixties resulted in the establishment of numerous Hispanic churches, especially along the eastern seaboard. In Miami alone there are now close to 100 Southern Baptist Hispanic churches. Since 1975, Southern Baptists have resettled over 10,000 refugees. To date 281 language-culture congregations have been established among them.

Another method for church-planting involves Anglo churches sponsoring ethnic congregations. Nueva Jerusalem in Houston, Texas is a case in point. Sponsored in 1979 by an Anglo church in a transitional community, this Hispanic group consisted of four families when it began its meetings. Today it has 250 members and around 300 in Sunday morning worship. The Anglo and the Hispanic congregations continue to meet in the same building and to share in its operating expenses.

Still another method that has been used is ethnic churches taking the initiative to start other ethnic congregations. For example, the Chinese Baptist churches in Houston and Memphis felt a mutual concern about starting a Chinese Baptist church in New Orleans. Together they provided the resources for a layman to travel to New Orleans on weekends. Today this 80 member congregation is moving rapidly to secure its own building.

Another factor in the indigenous approach used by Southern Baptists involves the training of ethnic leaders. The number of ethnic ministerial students in college and in Seminary has increased dramatically over the past two decades. This, however, does not remove the need for training in languages other than English. To meet this need, the Language Missions Division has established Ethnic Leadership Development centers in many parts of the country. These centers offer a Certificate in Christian Ministry, a Diploma in Theology/Religious Education/Music, and an Associate of Divinity degree. In addition to this, the Division relates to Baptist Colleges and Seminaries to assist them in the development of contextualized leadership training programs. For example, some of the seminaries are developing an ethnic track in the Doctor of Ministry and the Doctor of Philosophy programs.

Still another factor that has undergirded Southern Baptist Ethnic work has been the publication of contextual language materials designed to contribute to the spiritual development of the various ethnic groups. To meet this need, the Baptist Sunday School Board now has a number of highly skilled staff members representing the major ethnic groups in the country.

A factor that has contributed to the development of ethnic work while at the same time promoting a sense of oneness and belonging has been the inclusion of ethnic persons in the executive boards of the agencies of the Southern Baptist Convention. For example, the Foreign Mission Board and the Home Mission Board have had ethnic board members for a number of years.

Ethnic America is offering the Protestant denominations one of their greatest challenges today. Most of them seem to be facing up to this opportunity, but not without a struggle. Ethnic churches do not share the same national and religious history as their North Atlantic counterparts. This sometimes causes confusion, if not conflict in terms of identity and tradition and even doctrine and polity. Problems of intercultural communications are not uncommon. However, the positive aspects far outweigh the negative, and opportunities abound for new growth, spiritual vitality, and cross-cultural application of the gospel. The churches are being brought closer to the problems of a pluralistic world and the complex needs of its people, and they are therefore reaching out to all with a deeper compassion and a more meaningful and effective sharing of the gospel.

When the World Arrives on Your Doorstep

James Westgate*

Ethnic pluralism is probably the watchword of our day. Our cities are a constantly changing patchwork quilt. Now the pluralism is spreading to suburban areas as well. Most often a community is slowly introduced to a growing ethnic minority but sometimes an ethnic group takes a community by storm.

La Crosse, Wisconsin, is only a few miles away from a major army base. Several years ago 30,000 Cubans were flown in to Fort McCoy. A small town of 20,000 people suddenly had 30,000 Spanish-speaking refugees on their doorstep. Townspeople never considered that they would have a Hispanic "problem".

Such changes prompt questions:

How do we impact these people?
Are our churches ready to reach out?
If so, how?
What would be the consequences if we did?

Many denominations have been good at church-planting and starting ethnic churches. But how do we move existing churches through the transition of incorporating a growing ethnic population into their current congregations, and have them survive? With our society growing in its diversity, how do we prepare our churches for inevitable integration?

To focus on the ethnic transitions and tensions a church must undergo is to concentrate on only one area of change. The church is rarely stable. There are generational changes, for example, as a dominant age group grows older and not enough young people come into the

* Rev. Jim Westgate has pastored urban churches in changing ethnic neighborhoods for a number of years. He currently is a faculty member at Trinity Evangelical Divinity School.

church to fill the gap. There are economic changes when a city congregation moves to the suburbs and budget support disappears.

Another change occurs when members of the congregation move to the suburbs and identify with the church differently. The church changes its perception of them also because of a change in the level of their participation.

And ethnic and cultural change happens in the midst all of this. External changes can be stressful enough, but now others live near us who have a completely different orientation toward life. They have

When the world arrives on your doorstep...

different value systems and a different way of carrying out their daily activities. Their art forms are different and their music is different. They have a different work ethic and respect for property. All of a sudden they start impacting a community. They move in, and we realize that we are no longer able to hold the community together. That realization stimulates all sorts of questions: Can we survive? Where do we go from here?

To complicate the issue even more, different racial groups are accepted in different ways. Anglos tend to be more open to Asians and Hispanics than to Ethiopians. Some "middle-class, professional" Cubans are more acceptable than blue-collar workers. Even among racial groups there may be a hierarchy. Sometimes a Puerto Rican will buy a home or apartment and rent it to a Mexican. Let's examine the stages of transition an area will experience. These are from a book titled *Racial Transition in the Church* by James Davis and Woody White.

PRE-TRANSITIONAL STAGE

The pre-transitional neighborhood is one that has the most potential for change. Minorities may not yet have entered or they may be present in such small numbers as to be invisible. Their presence is not a factor in the community. If you'd like to see how your area had changed in the last few years, go to your library or city hall and ask for a DTF-3 Profile. It includes information about housing, economics and language, among other things. Comparing the 1970 and 1980 reports will reveal how much change has occurred.

EARLY TRANSITIONAL STAGE

The first few minority families may be welcomed or at least not resisted. When we think of the hundreds of communities that have changed over the last 30 years, we realized how few nasty incidents there have been. In the early transition stage, race relationships may be quite positive. Dominant and minority groups, often led by church members, may attempt to maintain a stable racially-mixed community. The more liberal and activist members of the community often mobilize the church, the PTA and neighborhood associations to maintain an interracial character. In the early transitional stage original residents may be aware of the presence of minorities, but most of them are calm and friendly.

LATE TRANSITIONAL STAGE

During the late transition a community or church may realize that it has lost its original identity. This is when political practices enter in. Often real estate sales encourage a flight to the suburbs. People begin to shop outside the community and economic disintegration begins.

POST-TRANSITIONAL STAGE

The post-transitional stage is a time of stability. If the time of reorganizing, if the time of settling down is after the major transition has taken place, it is time to begin to rebuild and stabilize the community. This is a good church-planting opportunity. There is much more risk in the late transition stage than in the post-transition stage. You either need to be there early and stay through the transition, having chosen your allegiances, showing you are going to be an open church, a church that is going to include other ethnic or racial groups, or you need to pull in behind as the community is in the process of stabilizing.

PRESSURES OF TRANSITION

There are time pressures. We are used to having instant success. There is going to be pain; no instant remedy exists for a church in transition. Congregations should understand that a three-to five-year adjustment period is necessary. Churches going through transition lose significant people along the way. It's a price that will have to be paid.

There are economic pressures. What demands will the new group bring? How should we continue to provide for the old group? There are denominational expectations. Headquarters leaders don't view folding churches positively.

RESPONSE TO TRANSITION

The response to transition is similar to grief. It begins with denial, as members of the congregation pretend that it will not happen. Anger follows and then bargaining or rationalization: "If only we could have a few more years. Buy a little more time so we don't have change." Depression sets in, often among the leadership. Fatigue and lack of energy spread. Finally renewal agents surface, and commitment is renewed. People can be found at various stages. Be aware of these stages and use them as points of discussion.

Another response is "fright and flight." Homeowners (or even the church) sell quickly and move before a major incident. Confrontation and resistance produce prejudice and racism. When we are threatened we will use our power to manipulate so that we survive. This is racism, and we need to be aware that it is alive and well in many of our churches.

Talking about the situation is an alternative response that will lead to more openness. It provides an opportunity to work through options. By studying the background of the new people, the congregation can be prepared for what to expect. By learning the culture, an appreciation can be developed for what the minority group has contributed historically.

There is even an option for the church that insists on closing its doors. In one case, the church closed, but turned its assets over to another church willing to plant an ethnic church. A new church was established, and the community was able to be reached despite the loss.

STRATEGIES FOR TRANSITION

When the time has come to prepare a church for transition, it is helpful to work through these steps to stay on the right track:

First, affirm the commitment by reviewing the biblical basis for the decision. Examine the church traditions in light of God's mandates. Ephesians 2 is a good reminder that all are fellow citizens with God's people. Diversity may not be comfortable, but it needs to be recognized as valuable in order to have a successful experience.

Second, define the corporate purpose. After the biblical foundation has been rebuilt, brainstorm about all the possibilities for the new ministry. Find out where the various members of the congregation will be willing to invest their time, energy and finances. A questionnaire is one way of doing this. The answers will reveal the priorities the congregation is willing to accept as well as give them the opportunity to ask questions and vent anxieties.

Third, create the reality of the situation. Define the ministry and make plans to implement it. This is often a crisis stage. For the first time many people are confronted with the incorporation of ethnics as a reality, not just a subject for discussion. Now is the time when most people leave the church, or they choose to cut back their participation. This calls for a long, hard look at the goals and mandates that have been the basis thus far.

Finally, go for it. Don't just be satisfied running programs. Give of yourself. In 1 Thessalonians 2:8 it says, "We gave you not the Gospel of God, but our very own soul." Bring the message and wrap it in a life. Stick the situation out, learn to appreciate the new culture and genuinely encourage and work with the newcomers. They may be as apprehensive as you are.

Ministry Among Newcomers

Alec Hill*

A decade has passed since Communist forces seized power in Vietnam, Laos and Cambodia. Vivid scenes come quickly to mind: the fall of Saigon, the "boat people," the suffering of Cambodia and the refugee camps.

Some 700,000 Southeast Asian refugees have resettled in the United States. How have they fared? What role has the evangelical church played in their resettlement? What strategies of evangelization and discipleship are being used?

The mission field has moved to us. Over 10 percent of the American households interviewed in the 1980 census spoke a language other than English in their homes. We are experiencing the largest wave of immigrants, refugees and undocumented aliens in 60 years. And these newcomers are not, like their predecessors, primarily Caucasian. They are Asian and Hispanic.

Typical Asian refugees are at least nominally Buddhist. In the country of their birth, they may have heard about Christianity, but probably never met a Christian. The upheavals which started in 1975 have left them uncertain and questioning. They arrive in the United States sponsored by a relative or an agency. The first lesson they learn is that materialism and eroticism are the two gods of American culture.

The magnitude of Christian involvement with these peoples may surprise some. Indochinese ministries have been established in every part of the country. Some are partnered with American congregations, others are more independent. Several denominations have developed national strategies to encourage such growth. Don Bjork, World Re-

---

*Alec Hill is an attorney and heads World Relief's refugee ministry in the Pacific Northwest.

lief's Associate Executive Director for Refugee Services, believes that "refugee resettlement may be America's most productive home mission endeavor for the 1980s."

A careful survey of refugees sponsored by evangelical churches indicates that 25 percent now consider themselves to be Christians. How can this phenomenon be explained? There are four possible answers.

First, the failure of Communism to fulfill its promises and of Buddhism to protect its own, have caused many to rethink their world view. Millions have died of starvation and disease or have been executed. Survivors are open to new ideas and beliefs.

Materialism and eroticism are the two gods of American culture

Second, the first people to greet many of the refugees arriving in the camps were Christians. The compassion shared by Christian nurses, teachers, college students and others has had a great impact on lives shattered by brutality and betrayal. At one point in 1980, there were more Cambodian Christians in one refugee camp (10,000) than there had been in all of Cambodia prior to 1975. Baptisms are still occurring at a rate unprecedented in the over 60 years of missionary activity in Vietnam, Cambodia and Laos prior to 1975.

Third, Americans have been mobilized to respond to the needs of refugees as they resettle in this country. Tangible actions such as sponsoring, moving furniture, and tutoring English are a great witness to the refugee who views the United States as a foreign and sometimes frightening land. Jesus' admonition in Matthew 25 to "welcome the stranger," to be a bridge to new life, is a challenge many lay people have accepted.

And fourth, church leaders believe that the Holy Spirit is making a special move among these peoples, particularly Cambodians. Raleigh Farrell, Assemblies of God National Secretary for Specialized Ministries, says: "There is no doubt that God is very active right now with the Indochinese. We are excited to be a part of that move."

Much of the numerical growth of these ethnic churches happens as they continue sponsoring more from their own countries. The principles of service evangelism apply here — credibility is built, the right to be heard is earned. The cycle starts over, with Indochinese Christians taking the lead this time. In California, where 40 percent of the Indochinese reside, many Vietnamese, Laotian and Cambodian pastors are using this method to build their congregations. These churches are located in cities such as El Cajon, Garden Grove, Whittier, Hacienda Heights, Riverside, Modesto, San Jose, San Francisco, Stockton and Sacramento.

Such a ministry model is predicated upon trained pastors. However, ordained Indochinese leaders are few in number. Of the 33 ordained pastors in Cambodia prior to 1975, only six survived the horrors of Pol Pot's Communist regime. Dara Pen, Christian and Missionary Alliance (C&MA) Director of Cambodian ministries, observes that "key strategies include Bible school training for aspiring pastors and lay evangelism. Without trained leaders, we cannot start new churches. It is the only way of the future."

Some ministries have not been able to wait for trained pastors. A C&MA church in Brooklyn, New York is an example. About five years ago, a Caucasian church was planted by Pastor George Reitz. His American congregation had grown to about 50 in 1981. When a Cambodian Christian came to church desiring to study the Bible, a Sunday afternoon service was soon started. Within three months of that first service, 90 Cambodians were attending regularly. Says Pastor Reitz, "The harvest is indeed plentiful, but the laborers are few. It is exciting but difficult to pastor two congregations at the same time." Four models of ministry are helpful for working with refugees:

1). Service evangelism.
2). Incorporating refugees within American congregations.
3). Partnering ethnic and American congregations.
4). Planting separate ethnic churches.

These models clearly overlap and are not mutually exclusive in nature.

Americans have been mobilized to respond to the needs of refugees as they resettle in this country

1. Service Evangelism
   Service Evangelism can be defined as those ministries which meet the physical, social, emotional and economic needs of the non-Christian. Done in Jesus' name, such activities build quality relationship and earn credibility for the believer. Authentic compassion involves the whole person.

God himself displays such concern: "God ... loves the stranger, giving him food and clothing" (Deut. 10:18,19).

Successful overseas missionaries have learned that they must address more than just the spiritual needs of they seek to reach. In the cross-cultural context, one must first earn the right to be heard. And such a right comes through service — meeting the most pressing needs of the non-believer. Hence, hospitals are built, wells are dug, orphanages established.

Moving furniture is a great witness

How then does this principle of service evangelism translate in the context of resettling Southeast Asian refugees in the United States?

How does one obey the admonition found in Leviticus 19:33, 34: "The stranger who lives with you shall be to you as the native among you, and you shall love him as yourself ..."?

The most obvious application comes in the form of sponsoring a refugee family.

Sponsoring includes: meeting the newly arriving family at the airport; providing temporary housing; ensuring enrollment in school;

instituting a job search; and providing the friendship necessary to bridge cultural and language gaps. It is purely a moral, not a legal, obligation. The first meeting at the airport can be a magic moment. A basis for a lasting friendship is often established immediately.

"Meeting the physical needs of the refugee develops a sincere bond of trust. Sharing our faith follows naturally. They are curious why we care so much," says Pastor Les Whitehead of Burien Free Methodist Church Seattle, whose 150-member church has sponsored 45 Laotians over the past four years.

Meet the newly arriving family at the airport

Likewise, Becky Mavredes of Richmond, Virginia's Southside Church of the Nazarene: "The key to our current 140-member Cambodian church was our willingness initially to meet the crises of the day — provide clothing, rides to the doctor, etc. Thankfully, we are past that now (the Cambodians now help each other to a large degree), but it provided an essential foundation of credibility."

Realizing the importance of sponsorship, several denominations have made concerted national efforts to encourage local church involvement. Included in that number are the Evangelical Covenant, Christian and Missionary Alliance, Southern Baptist, Christian Reformed, Free Methodist, Nazarene, Episcopalian, Lutheran, Presbyterian and Catholic churches.

2. Incorporating Within the American Congregation

This ministry model usually starts with sponsorship. A refugee family regularly attends Sunday service out of loyalty to the sponsoring church. Usually, only the refugee children (who are quickly learning English in public schools) understand the service; the adults are lost. Yet, they continue to attend.

At this point, the church may respond in one of two ways. Either a separate Sunday school class is created for the adult refugees (generally, Bible stories are taught as a means of learning English), or no action is taken and the family gradually slips away from the church. The latter situation occurs all too frequently. Many churches are simply not prepared to minister cross-culturally to the foreign-born. When the refugees disappear from the pew, there is a mixed feeling of concern and relief.

Several churches have adjusted their Sunday services to accommodate the newcomers. First Covenant of St. Paul has an active group of over 150 Hmong refugees.

Pastor Bill Peterson explains "we have baptisms regularly, whole families at once. It is like the New Testament." The Hmong have requested that they be a part of the American congregation, not formed into a separate group. "They want to assimilate, to be American. This is perhaps a unique situation that runs counter to textbook ethnic church-planting. They want to be with us," notes Pastor Peterson.

Oakland's Lakeside Baptist Church (General Conference) has a Cambodian interpreter in the pulpit each Sunday, and is praying for an Ethiopian to provide a similar service to the twelve Ethiopian refugee families in attendance. Other activities include: Sunday afternoon worship service in Mandarin Chinese; Laotian Bible studies on Monday and Tuesday nights; Cambodian Bible studies on Tuesday and Wednesday nights; a Sunday school Bible class using English as a second language. Of the 240 people who attend the church, more than a third are foreign-born.

3. Partnering/Symbiotic Relationship

A "symbiotic relationship" is a biological term meaning "the intimate living together of two dissimilar organisms in a mutually beneficial relationship."

Hence, the third ministry model involves two congregations, one American and one Indochinese, operating independently yet in partnership.

Such relationships involve much more than just co-locating in the same building. Joint planning of financial resources, volunteers and programs regularly occurs. In this manner, the refugee congregation enjoys both its cultural independence and the communal support of its American counterpart. Symbiotic relationships like this can be found in such diverse places as Portland, Oregon; Potomac, Maryland; and Garden Grove, California.

A prime example of such a relationship exists between Seattle's University Presbyterian Church and the Cambodian church it helped establish. During 1980-81, the American church sponsored several Cambodian families. A Sunday morning English class was started and about 25 Cambodians attended weekly. In late 1981, a handful of Americans, mostly lay people, decided that a small Cambodian church service should follow the English class.

The preaching was shared by four Americans who spoke through a Cambodian interpreter. The church grew from 25 to 125 in eight months. In January 1983 a Cambodian pastor relocated from Los Angeles. Sunday services are now operated completely by the Cambodians. However, American involvement continues through Bible studies, sponsorship and language help. States Pastor Tim Dearborn: "The development of local ethnic leadership is our highest priority."

Dallas's East Grand Southern Baptist Church has hired a Vietnamese pastor to minister to the large numbers of refugees being resettled in that area. The result is a separate Vietnamese congregation of over 100 regular attendees. As a member of the pastoral staff, Reverend Ha maintains vital links with the American church. He is convinced that the partnership works well: "The American church volunteers are most helpful. I preach and disciple, they help with the physical and social needs. Thank the Lord for active lay people. All I have to do is coordinate them."

Two other Seattle churches, Bethany Presbyterian and Japanese

Presbyterian, have assisted in the establishment of a Mien (tribal people from Laos) church of about 130 people. The Mien church has four functioning elders, all of whom were trained and discipled by American lay leaders. As the elders have taken more responsibility for the spiritual growth of the congregation, their American friends have been able to assist in other areas. For example, in 1982 economic needs became the paramount concern of the Mien community. Consequently American volunteers started a large-scale farm project and created a means to market the women's crafts. The former project is acknowledged nationwide as a model for successful refugee truck farming. Coordinator Cal Uomoto notes: "The key is to wait on the Lord for guidance. We are having the times of our lives learning about soil and marketing. None of us had any experience before."

4. Planting Separate Refugee Churches

A final ministry model involves the planting of independent ethnic churches. This model is particularly appealing for those denominations which had churches functioning in Vietnam, Laos and Cambodia prior to 1975. The two largest Protestant denominations operating under this model are the Christian and Missionary Alliance (C&MA) and the Southern Baptist Convention.

C&MA missionaries were first sent into Vietnam in 1911, Cambodia in 1923 and Laos in 1928. By 1975, it is estimated that C&MA churches had 175,000 members in Vietnam, 8,000 in Cambodia, and 10,000 Hmong in Laos.

National pastors were trained or being trained to take more responsibility. Likewise, the Southern Baptists entered Vietnam in 1956 and were heavily involved in planting Vietnamese churches and training national pastors.

Other groups similarly involved, though to a lesser extent, include the Swiss Brethren (Laos), Mennonites (Vietnam), an unaffiliated charismatic fellowship (Cambodia), and Campus Crusade for Christ (Cambodia).

Of course, the largest mission effort was conducted by the Roman Catholic church which sent its first missionary to Vietnam in the eighteenth century. In 1975, it numbered upwards of 10 percent of Vietnamese as members of its parishes.

The advantages that these denominations have in planting Indochinese churches in the United States are obvious: trained Indochinese leadership; appropriate literature; and years of experience in understanding cultural and religious values. The overseas sensitivity to culture continues here. States Dr. Fermin Whittaker, the Southern Baptist Director of Ethnic Church Growth: "Our goal is to evangelize, not Americanize. We are not attempting to make Americans, but to let each ethnic group express their faith in their own language. All of our 200 works with Indochinese are predicated on this premise."

In this model, Indochinese pastors report directly to a field director of their own ethnic group. Hence, Cambodian pastors affiliated with the Southern Baptist Convention in the United States report to Reverend Sok Thuong Doeung of Houston. Similarly, Reverend Yong Xeng Ang, C&MA field director of Hmong Ministers in Denver, has over 30 Hmong C&MA pastors and elders reporting to him. The largest Hmong church, in Fresno, California, has nearly 1,000 members. Most Indochinese congregations meet in American church buildings, often on Sunday afternoon when the sanctuary is available.

It is up to us, the church, to reach out to these persons. They are open and curious. Who will win their heart? Perhaps the greatest irony is this: We gave our offerings to send missionaries to Vietnam, Laos and Cambodia prior to 1975. The results were mixed. Now God has allowed these unreached peoples to come to us begging for our love and the true God's answers. Our response? As noted in this article, some truly exciting ministries are underway, but many needs remain unmet, and many opportunities untapped.

The ministry door will not be open forever. Within two years after arrival, refugees usually settle into the culture and either return half-heartedly to the faith of their ancestors or the goals of material prosperity. Will we respond to this opportunity in a prompt manner or wait until it is gone? The choice is ours.

Ministry Among Jews

Steve Schlissel*

"Selectavision" is not just a clever name for a popular videocassette recorder. It's also a good term to describe the process by which we scan, evaluate and absorb information, especially about our own and other ethnic groups. We tend to see what we want to see, know what we want to know, and, too often, believe what we want to believe.

Nowhere is the process more evident than in the historic relationship between Church and Synagogue. This "selectavision" must be recognized, addressed, and overcome before we can expect to see significant progress in our task of bringing God's ancient people into the body of Messiah.

In reporting on a management seminar we had attended, Bernard Stonehouse recalled the group was asked to look around the room for green objects. After a reasonable time, the facilitator asked the group to close their eyes and name red articles in the room. No one could name a single object, even though the room was filled with red things. If you lock onto certain perceptions, you will lock others out of the picture. For nineteen centuries, the Church of Jesus Christ has, by and large, locked onto reasons not to evangelize the Jews, and locked out the many good, scriptural encouragements to do so.

We have locked onto:

> *The Jews, who both killed the Lord Jesus, and their own prophets ... they please not God, and are contrary to all men (1 Thes 2:15).
>
> *As concerning the gospel, they are enemies for your sakes (Rom 11:28).

* Rev. Steve Schlissel is a converted Jew and ministers in Queens, New York.

*(They) fill up their sins always: for the wrath of God is come upon them to the uttermost (1 Thes 2:16).

*Behold, your house is left unto you desolate (Matt 23:28).

We have locked out:

*My heart's desire and prayer to God for Israel is, that they might be saved (Rom 10:1).

*As touching election, they are beloved for the fathers' sakes (Rom 11:28).

*Have they stumbled that they should fall? God forbid ... for God is able to graft them in again (Rom 11:11, 23).

*For the gifts and calling of God are without repentance ... And so all Israel shall be saved (Rom 11:29, 26).

Such studied "selectavision" on the part of the Church led to systematic anti-Semitism, as ideas became actions in history. Paul's caveat to the Gentiles, "Be not high-minded, but fear," was either ignored or forgotten as many became "wise in (their) own conceits" and provoked Israel to despair instead of jealousy. The Jews' very existence became a thorny theological problem for the Church which viewed itself as the true Israel and heir of all promises. The solution? "The Church ... appropriated blessings to herself and pointedly applied to the Jews the curses which the prophets uttered regarding Israel." Such a solution gave a theoretical green light to persecutions of the Jews which, to this day, remain the single largest obstacle to communicating the gospel of the Messiah. The Jews have "locked onto" the negative aspects of Church history and "locked out" the person of Christ.

Roderick Campbell put his finger on the problem when he wrote,

Perhaps the humbling truth is that Christendom has, in large, abandoned the kind of Christianity which the Bible proclaims, and those who turn away from the thing which they know as Christianity are wholly ignorant of what true Christianity really is. There is too much substance in the Jews' complaint that Christendom has hidden the face of Christ from them.

The following is a sampling of some of the acts behind which Christ was hidden from the Jews:

Year	Event
325	The Christian Church formulates its policy toward the Jews: Jews must continue to exist for the sake of Christianity in seclusion and humiliation.
1096-99	First Crusade. Crusaders massacre the Jews of the Rhineland. Many Jews commit suicide rather than submit to baptism.
1190	Anti-Jewish riots in England: massacre at York and in other cities.
1215	Fourth Lateran Council promulgates a canon requiring Jews to wear a distinguishing mark.
1290	Expulsion of the Jews from England.
1348-50	Black Death Massacres throughout Southwestern Europe as a result of accusation that Jews poisoned water sources of Christians. Bands of roving Christians called for a "holy" massacre of the Jews.
1421	270 Jews burnt at stake in Vienna.
1492	Expulsion from Spain.
1496-7	Expulsion from Portugal: mass forced conversion.
1516	Venice initiates the Ghetto, the first in Christian Europe.
1535	Massacre of Tunisian Jews.

Add to this the numerous incidents of the Blood Libel (the notorious allegation that Jews murder Christians in order to obtain blood for Passover and other rituals), the forced baptisms, humiliations without number, the burning of synagogues with Jews inside, the myth of the desecration of the host, pogroms, anti-Jewish publications, and many other crimes, often performed "in the name of Christ," and we readily understand how Jewish "selectavision" has locked onto the worst of the Church.

While modern Jews are for the most part unaware of the details, there is embedded in their consciousness the belief that the cause of their sufferings is Christianity. They trace the line of persecution right up to Hitler, who is thought by many older Jews to be a historically consistent Christian. That is why the conversion of Jews to Christianity is viewed as abhorrent and totally unacceptable, if not simply unimaginable. The antipathy is so deeply ingrained that many Jewish believers have difficulty saying the name "Jesus Christ" years after their conversion.

So it comes as no surprise that while distributing literature amongst the Jews, we are often asked how much we are getting paid. They just can't conceive of a Jew sincerely embracing the Christian faith — "Jews," we are told, "don't believe in Jesus." "Do your parents know you're doing this?" is a common question. Many older Jews pity us, thinking that we have been duped by "the Gentiles" into believing a lie. They think of Christianity as institutionalized Gentile-ism. I can understand their incredulousness.

As a Jew growing up in Brooklyn, I had the impression that the world was made up of two religious groups: Jews and Roman Catholics. Other denominations were simply Roman Catholics who had not yet attained self-consciousness; sooner or later they'd discover who they were. (When I became a Christian, one of my mother's first questions was, "Do you cross yourself?" referring to the Roman rite.) Christians were the people who worshiped three gods, needed idols to aid them, and required a mediator between them and God, whereas Jews required none.

In addition to these widespread misperceptions of Christianity and Christ, most Jewish people have an adamant anti-missionary mindset: they respect the right of others to follow their own religion and expect others to respect theirs. They regard both their sufferings and their tolerance of others as sort of a price paid for which they can demand an immunity from evangelism (which is considered by Jews to be inherently arrogant). Hence, the most frequently heard lament in our evangelistic efforts is, "Why don't you leave us alone?"

The answer, of course, is that we must obey God rather than people. We must reach them with the gospel. Not to do so would be sinful. O. T. Allis has noted that those entrusted with the gospel have often

by commission and omission excluded the Jews from

the Christian Church ... The early Christians were instructed, in their proclamation of the gospel, to begin at Jerusalem. Both Peter and Paul began with the Jew. But the Christian Church has for centuries ... begun with the Gentile, often completely ignoring the Jew, and during long periods of time never gotten to Jerusalem at all. This is a tragic and lamentable fact. It is a sin to be confessed and repented of ... the conversion of the Jew should certainly figure very prominently in all plans and programs for world evangelization.

But how can we go about it? In light of what's been said so far, isn't Jewish evangelism a futile enterprise? Emphatically no! While history can help us understand Jewish resistance, it does not alter our commission. Therefore, we must resist any attempt to make us feel guilty for obediently evangelizing the offspring of Jacob. When the Jews of this generation rightly point out that the guilt of the crucifixion ought not to be laid upon them, we must be quick to point out that the guilt of the crusades ought not to be laid upon us. Jesus Christ himself must be central in all our efforts.

And, as a matter of fact, there has never been a better time to present Christ. Local churches and denominations can now take bold strides in establishing programs that will reach into Jewish communities with the message of Messiah's love. This is because the grandchildren of the turn-of-the-century Jewish immigrants, who constitute the majority of American Jews, live in a spiritual vacuum. What has been said previously about older Jews, their mindset and prejudices, does not apply equally to the new generation.

A newsletter from an alarmed Rabbi estimated that the intermarriage rate of American Jews is approaching 47 percent. Eighty-two percent of Jewish children do not attend synagogue. There are "declining figures for congregational affiliation, for Hebrew school enrollment, and for membership in Jewish communal organizations."

This slackening of the hold of Rabbinic Judaism on the young has paved new inroads for the gospel into the Jewish community. Traditionally, Rabbinic Judaism served as the cohesive factor, uniting Jews in Diaspora. Wherever Jews were scattered, they were distinguished by their allegiance to the Sabbath regulations and dietary disciplines developed by the Rabbis (ostensibly based on Scripture). Such distinctions, along with severe social penalties for infractions, were necessary if the Jews were to maintain a separate identity in a largely hostile world. However, the benefits of American tolerance have rendered that need largely anachronistic. The anonymity and apathy of the cities to which the Jews flocked were catalysts in prompting the descendants of Orthodox Jews to question just what benefit was derived from the rigorous observance of regulations that were often difficult and tedious.

A shift of values, the State of Israel, cultural amnesia and post-holocaust disillusionment among modern Jews, spells "harvest field" to an alert and loving church. The president of a large Jewish mission has estimated that more Jews have come to Christ since 1967, than in the preceding millenium. Of the sixteen million Jews in the world today, probably more than 200,000 are believers and the number is increasing steadily and dramatically. Predominantly Jewish congregations can now be found from Hollywood to Haifa, and from Little Rock to London.

Yet, contrary to much popular opinion, the means that will be used most significantly to bring life to the children of Israel are not independent Jewish missions or the current Messianic Jewish movement. However God may use these, he has not abandoned his primary vehicle — the local church — especially as it is encouraged by evangelical denominations. That the local church must do the work is evident from the following considerations:

*It is the church's responsibility (Eph. 1:22; 1 Thes 1:8)

*It is too easy for Jews to dismiss Jewish mission efforts as the work of "meshumadim" (apostates from Judaism). Gentiles often get a fairer hearing.

*The character of the church is more consistent with the New Testament model when it is made up of Jews and Gentiles.

*Jewish centers of population in America are distributed in such a way as to make it impossible for any other organization except the local church to accomplish the task.

The thrust of Jewish evangelism now and in the near future ought to be less oriented to the Jew as a Jew, and more toward the Jew as a person with a need. This approach is suggested by the large-scale rejection of Jewish tradition by the new generation of Jews, and their assimilation in urban centers. Therefore, the task of the church in the 1980s is simplified: 1). Find out where Jews live, 2). Reach out to them as people, and 3). Bring them into congregations that are sound, sensitive, loving and fervent.

Of the six million Jews in the United States, one-third live in the metropolitan New York area. But there are 10,000 or more Jews in each of more than 50 U.S.cities.

Here are a few suggestions for reaching Jews with the gospel. First, prepare your congregation by teaching them about Jewish sensitivities and objections, and "proper" responses. You want to keep embarrassing mistakes to a minimum. Any Jewish mission can assist you with materials or instructors. You might consider having a Sunday school quarter devoted to the history of Church and Synagogue. Invite a local Reformed Rabbi to guest-lecture at one or two of the classes. (Afterward, suggest to the Rabbi that you trade opportunities to address your mutual congregations on specific subjects, such as "Atonement from a Jewish Perspective" and "Atonement from a Christian Perspective." You may get to preach the gospel in a synagogue by invitation! (Acts 13:15).)

With your congregation "sensitized" and encouraged, you can begin reaching out. Several cults in America, recognizing the spiritual need among Abraham's children, have recruited a great number of Jews. The exodus of young Jews from suburban homes to urban cults is of great concern for Jewish leaders and educators and is always a hot topic. Have a series of lectures and/or films at your congregation on the cults. Print up attractive handouts and have them displayed in the windows of local merchants. Public libraries in Jewish neighborhoods are good places to advertise: the space is free, and Jews, being voracious readers, frequent the local library.

Your handout should avoid anything that sounds as if you are specifically seeking to draw a Jewish crowd. After all, you are concerned about all people; you're simply promoting a series that is also of concern to Jews. The handout could read something like this: At the top is written "CULTS" in 3-inch letters, and under that is typed, "are a threat to you and your family. As part of our community education program, First Church will be holding a series of lectures in which the cults' tricks and tactics are exposed. You cannot afford to miss," etc., etc. This program will serve a threefold purpose: it will educate your community, reinforce the fact that there is a distinction between fervent biblical faith and cultic fanaticism, and give Jews and Gentiles the opportunity of hearing the gospel.

Depression is a problem that cuts across every line. We recently ran ads in a local publication offering a free booklet "that will really help." Seven of the eight respondents were Jewish. We sent them a tract by Jay Adams, "What Do You Do When You Become Depressed?"

Jewish people will respond to ads placed by individuals far more positively and frequently than they will to ads placed by institutions. It would be especially helpful if someone in your congregation has a Ph.D. The response portion of your ad in that case would read: Write to J. U. Philpot, Ph.D. (followed by the church's address). The person addressed should be the person to correspond with the inquirer. Even better would be a seminar on "Depression: Its Cause and Cure" given by a Christian counselor, preferably well credentialed. Publicize it heavily and well in advance (at least six weeks).

If you live in an area where there are many elderly Jews, a good service to the community and to the Lord would involve sponsoring a Health Fair which could be held in cooperation with a local hospital or clinic. As part of the Health Fair you could have lectures on "Living with Diabetes," or "Chicken Soup and the Common Cold." A prominent display of materials relating to spiritual health should be displayed. Get names and addresses and send follow-up letters informing the participants of your service schedule and programs. Write a personal note at the bottom of the letter, if you remember the person. Keep them on your mailing list.

Find a few retired men in the congregation who are handy around the house. Begin a program in which they, through the church, offer to do minor repairs for local Senior Citizens. Advertise through public service announcements in all local media (free). Have the youth groups of the church distribute flyers in apartment buildings and shopping centers in Jewish neighborhoods.

Rent a billboard in a Jewish neighborhood and put on it, "'The punishment that brought us peace was upon Him, and with His stripes we are healed' (Isaiah 53:5). For information or comments, call Alex

Rent a billboard in a Jewish neighborhood

Spangler at 555-5555." Use any Scripture which you think would be appropriate.

Make it your goal to glorify God, not simply to convert Jews. In my experience, Jewish believers have come to the Lord mainly through personal study of the Scriptures, particularly the fulfillment of Old Testament prophecies in Jesus. Therefore, make it one of your primary objectives to get the New Testament Scriptures into the hands of Abraham's offspring.

In sum, your outreach will consist of your church's addressing concerns of today's urban Jews from a biblical perspective. They will become aware of your church through advertisements and handouts that are worded in a general, sensitive, informational fashion, but placed in areas where Jews will see them. There are many missions and agencies that will be delighted to help you get your program off the ground.

The time has now come for the church to lock out the excuses of a past day, and lock onto the challenges and opportunities God is presenting to our generation. If we have to select a vision, let it be the one the Apostle Paul offers in Romans 11:15, "If Israel's rejection be the reconciliation of the world, what will their acceptance be but life from the dead?" With such a vision, the outworking of our burden is a joy.

Ministry Among Internationals

Stacy Carpenter Bieler*

There are many barriers to beginning and continuing friendships. Sometimes it is a scary thing to not know where to begin a friendship. Think of your close friends. How did you become friends? Perhaps your friendship grew through spending time with one another, sharing common interests, trusting and caring for each other, listening and depending on each other.

How do you keep friends? Usually by continuing to communicate, to share experiences, to tell them how much you appreciate them and for what reasons, even if these events take place irregularly.

The first barrier to beginning an international friendship is to confront our own wall of fear and hate. While we were growing up we learned to build this wall to keep out those who do not look or live like we do. To build international friendships we must dismantle this wall against those we were taught to fear and hate. Henri Nouwen says, "We have surrounded ourselves with a wall of fear and hostile feelings .... Our fears, uncertainties and hostilities make us fill our inner world with ideas, opinions, judgments and values to which we cling as to a precious property."

We need to recognize these (sometimes hidden) "bricks" of hostility in order to get rid of them. We can then begin to reach out and love people.

The second barrier to international friendships is our self-centeredness and our culture-centeredness. This barrier shows when we think or say, "My way is the right way or the only way," or "You are different which means you are wrong." It also shows in our assumptions and prejudices toward groups of people.

* Stacy Bieler is a staff member with Inter-Varsity Christian Fellowship and has developed an exciting ministry with Internationals.

There are several other ways this barrier is manifested:

First, we may not accept criticism of our country. Later we come to recognize that the priorities in other cultures (e.g., the family) may be more biblical than our own.

Second, we frequently want to be in the superior or controlling role. In the friendship we want to be the teacher instead of the student. We do not like looking stupid or inept.

We learned to build a wall to keep out those who do not look or live like we do

We also want to be the giver instead of the receiver. There is a saying, "Americans are great hosts and poor guests." Lederer and Burdick's book, *The Ugly American,* tells us how Americans are viewed overseas. We want to emulate the hero because he "was humble about everything and he made it clear that he thought he was getting more than he was receiving." Do not be afraid of learning or receiving.

We need to let go of our self-centeredness which urges us to feel superior and to control those around us. We can then begin to accept others, accepting our differences.

Our culture's love of independence and our society's craving for mobility are also barriers to close friendships. Very often we think it weak to lean on people and to trust them. We often do not know how to handle people caring for us. We protect ourselves, not wanting to give because we will get hurt when the relationship dissolves with the move of one of us.

This shallowness is probably the most frustrating aspect of American friendships for internationals. They usually come from a very small circle of friends where they do everything together and do not think anything of asking things of one another. Friendship is a great adventure and internationals have much to teach us. There are many examples of commitment and generosity.

In Italy, four boys went through school together. They chose the same college, found wives, and settled down together in the same town for the rest of their lives.

In South America you may tell your friend her piece of jewelry or some other object is beautiful. Since it brings you pleasure, she gives it to you.

When internationals come to the States, the one thing that they are interested in besides an education is an American friend. Most go home disappointed. They are bewildered by the outgoing friendliness of our "Hi, how are you?" when we do not slow down to hear their reply. We need to unlock our gate, taking the time to make friends. We will then find that we are often benefiting from the relationship more than they are!

The last obstacle to friendship is our impatience and pushiness in evangelism. We are used to instant pudding and immediate gratification. We are unused to counting the cost or being faithful when we do recognize the cost. We need patience, not programs, in our friendships. We need to see people as individuals, not feathers in our caps. Our friendships are a natural outcome of our faith in God and our love for humankind, not a tool to pull our friends over to "our side." As we witness to our new friends, we need to remember to speak "with gentleness and reverence" and "seasoned with grace ... responding to each person" (1 Peter 3:15 and Colossians 4:6).

An international's decision-making process is often different from ours. They may take longer in deciding because they are considering the cost more than we might. There may be a greater cost (persecution, rejection from families, possible death) for their decision back in their own country.

We need to remember that we befriend and share; the Holy Spirit convicts and converts. Our role is big enough — we do not need to take on the Spirit's as well.

Some of the greatest, most profound things that happen in peoples' lives are hidden. We need to reject impatience that can cause us to doubt our own abilities or fail to recognize God at work in the lives of friends. We can then be faithful in our work and in our expectations for God.

Though the barriers are great, God is greater still. As Ephesians 2 tells us, Jesus Christ is the great barrier-breaker between God and humans and between Jews and Gentiles. Verse 16 summarizes the first ten verses, "(That he) might reconcile us both to God in one body through the cross, thereby bringing the hostility to an end."

Jesus broke down barriers between a holy God and sinful people. Verse 14 summarizes the last twelve verses, "He himself is our peace, who has made the two one and has destroyed the barrier, the dividing wall of hostility." It is almost impossible to understand how great a barrier there was between the Jews and Gentiles. Social, religious and historical barriers are not new for Jesus! He who has done such a great work is able and eager to help us now with the barriers we face.

Here are a few practical suggestions that may help you in beginning and maintaining a significant friendship with an international:

First, ask God to guide you to a person you will like. People from other cultures may seem intimidating and fearful. They may look, dress and speak differently, but most often they have the same dreams, feelings and questions about life as we do. Also, ask God to give you the courage to begin conversation and initiate the friendship.

It is important to be aware of some guidelines as you begin your encounter. Ask questions, but do not control the conversation. And do not be afraid of silence. Ask their name, and repeat it until you can say it correctly. You may even want to write it down.

Don't worry about feeling foolish when actually you're being interested. Rather than asking them their impressions of America, focus on what they miss about their country. The way you relate to an international in conversation can encourage their openness toward you. Speak distinctly, not too quickly, and don't use slang. Do not speak louder — their hearing is probably fine. Do not become impatient.

In addition, don't set yourself up as superior to them. Adopt an attitude of learner; educate yourself about their culture as they are trying to do with yours. There are several ways to do that:

— Buy a world map
— Read about their country in an encyclopedia
— Follow their country in the news
— Experience a foreign film together
— Accompany them to their cultural events
— Discuss issues your two countries share in common

Don't be afraid to share your faith. You are not alone; God has gone before you. If your faith is an integral part of your life, it can come up naturally in conversation.

Wisdom is needed when questions are raised about the United States being a "Christian country." Internationals often become confused and angry about our nation's racism, materialism and militarism. That can be an opportunity to share how our faith is both individual decision of the heart and a corporate responsibility to change our surroundings.

The wall of fear and hate can be dismantled brick by brick. We can open our locked gate of independence and mobility and let ourselves depend on others. Finally, we can exchange our obstacle course of impatience and pushiness for a straight path of patience and sensitivity. What a privilege it is to be a part of God's plan for reconciling all things to himself!

Ministry Among
American-Born Chinese
Gail Law*

To the Chinese churches in North America the decades of the 1960s and 1970s were characterized by unprecedented growth. The number of Chinese churches rose from 66 in 1955 to 468 in 1982. However, careful study of the growth statistics reveal that the large majority of the conversion and transfer growth were confined to overseas born Chinese (OBC, for short) who had immigrated to the country or studied here on student visas. If "reaching somebody with the gospel" is defined as their acceptance of Jesus Christ as Lord and Savior, and their incorporation into the fellowship of his Church, then the American born Chinese (ABC, for short) is one of the most unreached peoples in the country. The 1980 U.S. census shows that about 40 percent of the Chinese are ABC, but they constitute only 22.4 percent of the congregation in the Chinese churches. Few are represented on the church board — even fewer have made it to the pastorate.

For about twelve years various Chinese church leaders, especially the few prominent ABC among them, have expressed their concern over the evangelization of the ABC. Seminarians have written many papers and a few dissertations on the same issue. Under the spirit of NACOCE '78 and the leadership of four ABC leaders, the Fellowship of American Chinese Evangelicals (FACE) was formed with the specific purpose to address the problem. In spite of all these efforts, reaching the ABC with the gospel remains one of the "toughest nuts" to crack. Based on a literature survey of the ABC and interviews with 40 OBC and ABC pastors and lay leaders in North America, exploration has begun on the issue from the viewpoint of leadership training and mission strategy.

* Dr. Gail Man-wah Law is a prominent researcher both in Hong Kong and in the United States and is a member of the Strategy Working Group of the Lausanne Committee for World Evangelization.

UNDERSTANDING THE ABC.

To the outsiders, the ABC is a homogeneous people group. In reality there is a wide range of heterogeneity and a lack of cohesiveness among ABC. Roughly speaking, the ABC can be categorized into three age-groups according to the period in which their parents immigrated to the country. The years of 1943 and 1968 are of special significance in terms of population size and the sociological makeup of Chinese immigrants before and after those years. Before 1943 the U.S. government reinforced the Chinese Exclusion Act, so very few Chinese women were allowed to join their husbands in the U.S. from Asia. The population size of the ABC born before 1943, now aged 41 or above, is relatively small.

In 1943, President Franklin D. Roosevelt signed the "Act to Repeal the Chinese Exclusion Acts" and began a period (1943-1968) in which Chinese women trickled into the country. Even then, the immigrant quota was set at 105 per year, including men, women and minors. The ABC born in this period now aged 16 to 41, form a larger population. As of July 1, 1968, each independent country outside of the Western hemisphere was granted an immigrant quota of up to 20,000 per year. With successive revision, today the country is absorbing annually 20,000 Chinese born in China, another 20,000 born in Taiwan and 6,000 born in Hong Kong, making a total of 46,000, in addition to those Chinese from the Philippines, Singapore, Malaysia and other parts of Southeast Asia. The largest population of ABC are now under 16 years old.

These age groups are important when they are studied in the light of their socioeconomic background. The U.S. immigration policy of each period not only determined the quota of the Chinese immigrants, but also the kind of immigrants who could settle in the country. It therefore also directly determined the sociological makeup of the parentage of the ABC of each period. Parentage governs such factors as home dialects, education, skills, profession, residence, types of homes, attitude towards Christianity and distance from the American culture, all of which are important.

Generally speaking, the early immigrants were mainly from the villages of Kwantun Province, and they settled as the Chinatown enclaves in the country. But with successive attempts to relax the stringency of the immigration policy and the escalating turmoil in

Asia, the sociological "mixes" of the later immigrants became increasingly complex. Today, in addition to the professions typified by the Chinatown enclaves, we find Chinese immigrants who are skilled technicians, highly-trained professionals, well-to-do business people who make their homes in high-cost suburban areas. A minority of them even speak English as the heart language with one Chinese dialect as the second language. The younger ABC generations are born into families of this complex mosaic of distinct sub-groups.

To compound an already complex picture, two other factors steadily exert their effects upon the changing mosaic.

First, the studiousness of the Chinese people and the priority they give to education greatly affect their upward social mobility. There has been a trend to move away from Chinatowns to settle in the suburbs. This move is usually accompanied by a move closer to the American cultural values.

Second, with each wave of incoming immigrants, there were young children who came with parents to settle in their adopted country. Technically they are OBC. But because of their upbringing in the American school system, they are culturally closer to the ABC than their OBC parents.

For a comprehensive understanding of the complexity of the ABC mosaic and its implications on evangelism, we must rely on the expert opinion of Christian anthropologists, psychologists and sociologists, in addition to biblical scholars, theologians and missiologists. The study of ethnic migrants and their descendants in the U.S. is a new discipline.

The study of Asian Americans (including Chinese, Japanese and Koreans) shares certain things in common with other ethnic studies in that it lacks a defined perspective, a body of theory and a definite object for study. Before a fuller body of knowledge is available to us, we must at least work with the following understanding, which provides an answer to the question, "What is the ABC like?":

1). The largest majority of the ABC is under the age of 41.

2). The first sizable population of ABC are college-age and young adults.

3). ABC and OBC as technical categories referring to their places of birth may not be helpful to mission strategists. Places of birth create problems for evangelism insofar as they affect the cultural world view of the persons involved. A more functional category for our consideration will be "cultural OBC," meaning Chinese in world view.

4). The dichotomized or bipolar concept of ABC/OBC commonly adopted by the Chinese churches is true insofar as it is applied to their places of birth. But it becomes misleading when it is used to imply their cultural orientation. A more realistic and less misleading concept would be the "continuum concept" with "cultural OBC" on one end and "cultural ABC" on the other. The majority of the technical ABC and technical OBC are found somewhere in between. Moreover, people tend to change with the society they live in. Most Chinese are moving along the direction towards "cultural ABC." This continuum concept is pertinent and important to the mission strategist.

5). The largest majority of the ABC are first generation children born to immigrant parents. When the parents join the church, their local born children who are culturally more ABC than they are must be accommodated. Every church planted among Chinese people must be sufficiently bicultural to accommodate many who are at different stages along the "cultural ABC/cultural OBC continuum" and are moving at different paces towards the end of "cultural ABC."

THE OUTREACH EFFORT

The majority of the Chinese churches in the U.S. were planted as immigrant churches and are pastored by cultural OBC pastors. However, most of them do try to accommodate the ABC through their church programs. The most effective program to bring ABC children into the church is the Saturday morning Chinese school. Immigrant OBC parents want their children to learn some Chinese and are only too willing to send them to the church on Saturdays.

From these Chinese classes, the ABC children are introduced to the junior fellowships and Sunday school, in which the instruction medium is English. Most of the counselors and teachers are OBC, and in some larger churches with longer history of existence, ABC counselors and teachers are also available. Starting from junior or senior high school, depending on the churches, the ABC youths are required to attend Sunday worship services. Most churches have Chinese sermons translated into the English language. Some have separate

Chinese and English services.

The larger and richer Chinese churches also seek to accommodate the needs of the ABC through team leadership. A small minority have ABC assistant pastors. A few churches even have ABC serving as senior pastors.

An honest evaluation of the outreach effort to the ABC reveal that only little success has been achieved. For the past 20 years the immigrant Chinese churches have learned that the ABC children are "accessible" but not "keepable." Though literally tens of thousands of ABC children have attended the Sunday school, most of them leave the church in their adolescent years or soon after that.

A common complaint from the local borns is that they are a minority in the larger society of the OBC-dominated church. They are not seen, not heard and not even an issue. Their needs are overlooked. They are rarely asked to assume positions of responsibility which would affect the policy and decision-making processes of the church.

There is a tendency for the dominant group to maintain the status quo rather than make changes to accommodate the small minority. The sermons of the OBC pastors are hard to understand, even when translated. Regardless of translation, an OBC pastor's sermon has many Chinese elements incorporated into it. The thoughts, humor, use of proverbs, basic philosophy and mode of communication of the OBC pastor are all oriented towards the cultural OBC. Few ABC can identify with such sermons. On the other hand, the OBC leaders are not without complaint against the ABC. To the people-oriented Chinese eye, the individualistic ABC are radical, disobedient, unstable, unreliable, unspiritual, rude and immature.

Recently, some success has been found by the larger and richer churches which are able to support team ministry staff with both ABC and OBC pastors serving in the same church. Interviews with these ABC pastors (including cultural ABC, being overseas born) reveal certain measures of success. They stand as leadership figures with whom the cultural ABC can identify. They are a channel of the minority's voice in the church. Very often they have to develop a certain kind of leadership style acceptable by the ABC.

The format of worship services, fellowship meetings and other church activities for the English speaking ABC are quite different from the Chinese speaking OBC section. However, the challenge facing these ABC pastors is how to help the OBC congregation see the validity of their type of leadership and approach to ministry which may be different from what they are used to. Fortunately, in most cases, the senior OBC pastors are very supportive.

Who should reach the ABC? It seems that the successful churches are those which provide leadership of two cultures. Those which fail are those which are unable to do so. The following facts must then be recognized in terms of appropriate leadership or worker.

1). Having the language does not necessarily mean having the culture. Chinese sermons translated word for word into English are not English sermons.

2). The individualistic ABC need leaders whom they can identify with.

3). Leadership appropriate for the culture implicates at least the person's leadership style, the way of communication, the process of thinking, the standard for evaluating good or bad and the approach to manage conflicts. It is in these areas that the people-oriented cultural OBC and the individual-oriented cultural ABC are divergent from each other, causing much misunderstanding.

4). The richer churches can provide bicultural leadership through team ministry. But the small churches need to have leaders who are sufficiently bicultural to accept the challenge.

This preliminary study shows that biological growth does not come naturally with the immigrant Chinese churches. Establishing the first ABC generation in the church is a type of pioneer mission. Although both OBC and ABC are ethnic Chinese, there exist various degrees of cultural distance between them. For one to reach the other requires training.

The key to success in reaching the ABC with the gospel lies in the provision of bicultural leadership which can keep them in the fellowship of the church. The bicultural leader has to impart bicultural perspectives to the OBC and ABC congregation in the same church; this is an unavoidable reality for the Chinese at this stage of development. One must be able to see the validity of both cultural ABC (American) and cultural OBC (Chinese) world views, and when in conflict, be able to critique each in the light of the Bible.

The Chinese churches have focused their ABC outreach among children. The Saturday morning Chinese school is an effective entry to the group and should be used. However, the church should provide bicultural training for Sunday school teachers, youth counselors and other types of workers who may deal with these children.

Church life will then be more relevant and interesting to the ABC. On the other hand, the ABC should also receive bicultural training so that they can have a better grasp of their identity both as Chinese and Americans. Such bicultural perspectives would also reduce the cultural distance between the ABC and the OBC of the church, thereby reinforcing unity in diversity.

Ministry in New York City

J. D. Golden*

The amazing thing about the church of Jesus Christ is that it will grow in some of the most adverse circumstances. Our responsibility is to increase our effectiveness in order to become better harvesters. Therefore, we need to be alert to what the Spirit of God is doing.

In New York City, we allowed the contents of the wineskin to determine the shape of the structure. It is self-defeating to force new wine into old wineskins. The same is true about using irrelevant methods to evangelize new peoples.

People must be evangelized in groups. They must not be seen only in a geographical setting. For example, in New York City, we were responsible for a nine-county area, having a population of nearly 17 million, with a high number of recent immigrants. This area also has the highest percentage of foreign-born residents in the nation.

Metropolitan New York City is interesting in that it is the only regional area of the United States with a movable boundary. The sphere of influence of the city reaches to Long Island and into New Jersey and Connecticut. If the emphasis were upon geography, evangelism would not be able to follow the people.

The following are steps we used in New York City:

AREA PROFILE

For our situation, the first step in evangelism was to see the city as God saw it. The area is made up of people, but people tend to cluster in groups. Therefore, we examined the city from a cultural perspective. The questions we had to address were: How many cultures,

---

* Overseer J. D. Golden is a seasoned urban pastor and worked in a significant church-planting effort in New York City.

where were they located, and what numbers?

EVANGELISM ANALYSIS
We set out to learn whether or not the area was ripe for evangelism. After fruitlessly attempting to establish churches, we wondered if God was still working in this area. This prompted the following questions: Where were other churches going, were they growing, and what kind of things were they doing? We used the best sources we could find and assembled an analysis of the area. This data impressed us, but we discovered that most of the information we needed was not in the computer, but out on the streets where the people were. We realized we should take to the streets to feel and see the heartbeat of the city.

On the streets we saw some storefront churches. Some groups were meeting in homes, and others in small cramped quarters for worship. This revealed to us that the church was indeed alive, but due to circumstances, it had taken on many different forms. The government structures were appropriate for the different needs, and the time schedules were accommodating the lifestyles of those attending.

A. WE WORKED WITH WHAT WAS WORKING.
Of the many groups of people, we discovered that some churches were multiplying while others had no growth. Sometimes, the different growth and non-growth groups were located in the same geographical area. We structured our work to fit the pattern. We became facilitators. We made it our task to support and aid the workers from the many cultures who had a simple desire to reach their people.

Locating proper facilities was a difficult and discouraging part of the growth process. Using whatever facilities were available was necessary until a permanent place of worship could be found. The Old Testament pattern of tabernacle served as an example. The people had to use what tabernacle or mobile facility they had until their temple or permanent place of worship could be built. Sharing of these facilities was a common practice in New York City: one church's temple served as another's tabernacle. Sharing the cost of the building can benefit in consolidating funds.

Another approach involved the "skyscraper missionary" — a family planted in a building or community to gain access to the area or the use of a room in such a building. This helped us to establish a base from which to work. This family's major emphasis was to meet people and witness in this station.

B. WE USED PEOPLE GROUPS.

We saw that people tended to remain in cultural groups. Even when they were separated geographically, they would travel considerable distances to maintain group ties. The congregational models we worked with always evolved along these cultural lines.

EXAMPLES OF ETHNIC GROWTH
THE ITALIAN CHURCH

This church started in an Italian community consisting of people in the lower income group, many of whom were on welfare. The educational level was very low.

In the beginning, a group of about seven people assembled to-

Using whatever facilities were available was necessary until a permanent place of worship could be found

115

gether. The church began in a home, and the people met in the middle of the week. Plans were eventually laid for the growth of the church.

There was a difference of opinion between the Director of Evangelism and Italian pastor about where they should establish their first church. The Director of Evangelism wanted to purchase a mobile chapel. The pastor insisted on a storefront. Even though the Evangelism Director believed the mobile unit was more contemporary and prestigious, the pastor's wishes for a storefront were observed. The church grew almost immediately. Today, the people have built a new building and expanded once. The attendance is approximately 500. They do not focus on Sunday school, and their largest attendance is on Friday evening rather than Sunday. There is a great emphasis on God's ability to supply their needs as well as on signs, wonders and miracles.

THE HAITIAN CHURCH

Due to the experience of Haitians with voodoo, there is a strong emphasis on the power of God. Their assumption is that if God is not stronger than voodoo, then they will not believe in him. They must be able to feel the power of God. Their singing is very lively and loud, and the worshipers become totally immersed in the worship.

This particular ethnic model is not measured by the facility but by the approach to worship and outreach. The building is usually a storefront. The ministry is powerful with demonstrations of the Spirit. Since their kinship link is very strong, they concentrate on reaching their own people.

When there is a need to begin a new church, the pastor calls all the people together for prayer and preaching. They select the most qualified people from among the congregation, lay hands on them and send them forth.

If the church is worshiping in a home, the Haitians make arrangements to rent a facility large enough to house a larger gathering. Haitian believers from all over the area come together to worship because they recognize the local group and have a great time of fellowship. When they leave, a large offering is received to get the church on its feet.

The pastors of the local church gather once a month for Bible study and prayer. During the service, communion is observed and leadership is recognized and encouraged. When several churches have been started, they are grouped into a district and given the challenge of planting new churches. When each district is established, the process repeats. After several districts are in operation, the entire culture then begins to assemble together for a giant celebration. With this sequence of events, a new level of excitement is obtained.

These are some ways ethnic churches can start and grow in cities. If we can understand urban wineskins and the cultural shapes they take in different places, ethnic evangelism can be encouraged and nurtured with increasing fruit. Be prepared for new wineskins and remember that they may not look like the old patched ones!